KILOBASE BUCHAREST A-Z

D1721641

edited by
Kilobase Bucharest
(Sandra Demetrescu
& Dragoș Olea)

PUNCH

Descrierea CIP a Bibliotecii Naţionale a
României
Kilobase Bucharest A-Z /
ed.: Sandra Demetrescu, Dragoş Olea. -
    Bucureşti : Punch, 2020
    ISBN 978-606-95055-1-9
I. Demetrescu, Sandra (ed.)
II. Olea, Dragoş (ed.)
7

CONTENTS

THE MANY KEYS
TO THIS ALPHABET BOOK
Sandra Demetrescu & Dragoș Olea

The old adage that "good things come to those who wait" perfectly describes what the making of this publication means to us.

The starting point of the project was the creation of KILOBASE BUCHAREST (2010) by Dragoș Olea and Ioana Nemeș (1979-2011) as a hybrid initiative somewhere between experimental artistic project, nomadic gallery and curatorial platform.

The first volume of KILOBASE BUCHAREST was produced in 2011 as part of the group exhibition *Image to be projected until it vanishes* curated by Mihnea Mircan at MUSEION Bolzano (IT)[1] and included the first eight letters of the alphabet, from A to H. Our decision to start the activity of KILOBASE BUCHAREST with a publication series, conceptualised as an experimental alphabet book, was intended as a homage to a city that inspired the genesis of KILOBASE.

The disappearance of Ioana in the same year determined the suspension of the editorial project for an indefinite period, and for emotional reasons the next two volumes did not materialise.

6

1   *BUCHAREST A-H* was produced and distributed internationally by the MUSEION museum (Bolzano) and Mousse Publishing (Milan), and at the invitation of several curators it was presented in the following exhibitions: *Image to be projected until it vanishes*, MUSEION, Bolzano, Italy, *LE CATALOGUE ET SES HYBRIDES* #1, École des beaux-arts, Toulouse, France (both in 2011), *LE CATALOGUE ET SES HYBRIDES* #2, Le Moinsun, Paris, France, *LE CATALOGUE ET SES HYBRIDES* #3, l'École Nationale Supérieure d'Art de Nancy, Galerie NaMiMa, Nancy, France, *invisible transfer of signals (for ioana nemeș)*, ArtPoint Gallery, Kulturkontakt, Vienna, Austria (all in 2012), Vienna Biennale—*Mapping Bucharest: Art, Memory, and Revolution* 1916–2016, MAK Museum für angewandte Kunst, Vienna, Austria (2015).

While forever fascinated with Bucharest, it never felt right to hit restart for *KILOBASE BUCHAREST A–Z* before the nightmarish 2020. During the months of confinement, when chaos and feelings of despair fluctuated with lengthy halts and intense reconfigurations, our longing for all things we cherish and loathe in the city reached unprecedented heights. Time to address a love letter of sorts to Bucharest.

In the almost ten years since the first publication, Bucharest has undergone a series of substantial transformations, yet its identity remains equally fragmented and notoriously difficult to capture and define.

In 2020 the KILOBASE BUCHAREST book resumed its A to Z trajectory, inviting twenty-six authors to create new content for this multi-layered publication.

Each author was invited to choose a letter of the English alphabet and a key word abstracting a facet of Bucharest that would serve as a base for developing a contribution. Thus, the publication is a polyphonic set of perspectives on a city capturing the imagination and interest of many artists, architects, writers and researchers.

Through artistic contributions plus a special insert—*I'm Telling You Stories. Trust Me* by the late artist Ioana Nemeş—as well as three reprints from the first publication united under the "&" symbol (the ampersand was for a long time considered a letter of the British alphabet), *KILOBASE BUCHAREST A–Z* dismantles many clichés and preconceptions about the city. Unexpectedly twisting every step of the way, the book is simultaneously passionate, melancholic, liberating, abstract, hyperrealistic, idealistic.

KILOBASE BUCHAREST A–Z is a publication, but also a multitude of other things.

*) The above-mentioned alphabet structure renders the publication a tool of sorts: a way to learn about and from Bucharest.

It's an *abc* attempting to conjure that difficult *love at first sight* feeling for beginners in all things Bucharest. Or it's a wealth of reasons, many unsung until now, for Bucharest willing connoisseurs to refresh their relationship with the city.

**) It is also an (incomplete) puzzle made of mirrors, magnifying glasses and metaphors.

Beautifully uncanny and tangled up, this colourful patchwork is capable of morphing with each reading, sometimes demanding another plunge for clarifications and drifts between contradictory emotions. The contributions are an eclectic mix of visual art, personal narratives, fiction, photography, critical texts and essays, performance documentation, artistic and anthropological research, new directions for hybridising local artistic and cultural practices, architecture and urban studies, economy and social context, queer life, sounds specific to Bucharest, nature as a metaphor for radical change, desires and speculations about the future of the city, and personal mythologies.

***) It is also the key to the city.

Most accurately, *KILOBASE BUCHAREST A–Z* is in fact a key chain with thirty-three such keys, entrusting with and bestowing upon *the curious* a multitude of entry points to the depths of Bucharest: a city that has never been walled, unlike those places where the tradition of the key to the city emerged. On the contrary, the open geography made it easily permeable to numerous layers

of influences and chaotically sedimented complexities. Difficult to crack and comprehend, to understand Bucharest one needs to be given such keys.
In all their diversity, the contributions are creating a network of common threads and loose ends that pin down a polymorphic version of the city, stretched between a somewhat diffuse past and its bursting becoming, waiting to be unlocked.

AMAR-AMĂRÂT / Key no. 1, Irina Bujor's contribution feels like a parting gift they received not long after moving abroad, disillusioned with the lack of opportunities in the city.

In the context established by artist Irina Bujor, AMAR-AMĂRÂT could be loosely translated as a sort of Eternal Downhearted-Bittersweetness. It defines, through a polysemantic extension, the unexpected encounter with a set of vintage objects: semi-broken, bearing the traces of production errors, incomplete. While also conveying a deeply local experience, something bound to happen almost exclusively in a certain place in Bucharest, where this category of objects has been defined.

Inexplicably for some, they managed to function as an ingredient for total transformation, soothing Irina's relationship with the city. In her take, there is no better description for the spirit of Bucharest than one of these AMAR-AMĂRÂT objects, sneaking into our hearts to heal emotional breakdown by means of their bittersweetness and through the cuteness of their faults, which makes them utterly unique.

Key no. 2, delivered by photographer Serioja Bocsok under the name BUZEȘTI, carries a weighty sense of loss following the terrible demise of the iconic Matache

Market building alongside several other edifices on a foggy night in November, a few years ago. The beautiful images he spontaneously took that night, together with a rather hesitant mind-map, are cinematic props for his (and our) fading memory of the timeworn charm exuded by Buzești street before gentrification and shady urbanistic plans kicked in.

studioBASAR, architects Alex Axinte and Cristi Borcan, delivers us two keys.

Key no. 30, titled BETWEEN, is available under the "&" symbol towards the end of the book, as a reprint of their contribution in the initial KILOBASE BUCHAREST A–H. BETWEEN is building towards an emotional and intellectual turn. The first part is about the innocent and unmediated-by-architectural-knowledge experience Alex and Cristi had of Bucharest in their childhood, during their first encounters with the capital as visitors, living in a city one hour away. While the second part is a selection of a few recent architectural interventions using the search-and-rescue methodology developed by them after starting to work together as studioBASAR.

They also deliver Key no. 3, COMMONING. Their 2020 contribution to the book presents in quintessential mode—short texts and complex narrative graphics—the conclusions of their most advanced and refined models of working with the community, in grassroots attempts to rebuild public spaces like the community library and the city school.

After a decade of studying the city from a multitude of perspectives, the evolution in their practice and intricate ways of engagement with(in) Bucharest become all the more striking. Fueled by aims of inclusion, empowerment, social justice and equality, their collective dreaming feels both progressive in imagining tools for the production of public and community spaces and an attempt to unearth what was best in terms of vernacular ideas shaping a community feeling during socialism.

While most of the book is dedicated to first-hand encounters with the city during the present and recent past, we also felt the need to commission contributions looking into the future.

One of these plunges aims towards a desirable unknown—DAYDREAMS brings together sets of wishes for the future of the city deposited in three different keys. From the desire to look at the city as a social organism that can be healed through processes of collective imagination, where change is not mandatorily massive and futuristic, but shaped by pragmatic solutions and heartfelt ideas, as articulated by curator Iuliana Dumitru in ONE THING TO WISH FROM/ FOR BUCHAREST/ Key no. 4; to CITY OF WITCHES AND WISHES / Key no. 5 by architect Ștefan Ghenciulescu, who starts by wondering how this is all possible. His reasonable explanation—witchcraft—is then twisted into a plea for a future city, glowing a bit more as a social sphere under new collective spells by invoking both decision makers and quasi-magical specters of positive change. Also adding to the daydreams is our own short wish-list— KILOBASE BUCHAREST / Key no. 6—for a design revolution concerning official public communication, in which to subversively incorporate an honest rediscovery of aesthetic gregariousness specific to the local spirit. Quotable, aching with empathy, unafraid of prettiness, these daydreams turned real would make a lucky Bucharest.

A different kind of otherworldly comes with Key no. 7 / EUROPA ON MAGIC

Can Europa—not the continent, but the not-so-stellar shopping complex—become a landmark for learning something unexpected about Bucharest? Apparatus 22 bets on this. Inspired by the rules and impulses of that unique micro-context on the outskirts of the city, the art collective pens a series of four riddles, one of their signature ways of asking persistent questions. Placed on images that feel like samples of pulp reality, the impossible riddles are open mental landscapes situated between visceral and radical fictional constructions. Charming and frustrating, immediate and esoteric alike, these riddles talk about informal economy, democratisation of design and the currents and undercurrents that shaped the place for years and years. Apparatus 22 also delivers Key no. 31 in a reprint from KILOBASE BUCHAREST A–H. The ERSATZ ECONOMICS intervention was inspired by the larger-than-life claim of H&M's advertising campaign when opening its first stores in Bucharest, back in 2011: "This city is about to change". Working with metaphors and narratives gathered from non-academic sources—press cuts and popular knowledge—Apparatus 22 built its own story on economics around the massive change in the streets and fashion scene of Bucharest as it occurred with the arrival of the mega retailer of mass-fashion.

With FRIENDS / Key no. 8, writer Mihnea Mihalache-Fiastru is submerging us in some of the harrowing realities of life in big cities by giving us direct and personal access to one of Bucharest's first communities of heroin addicts. Rather than telling their individual stories of substance abuse, the mix of poignant images and text works as a fable of friendship that is strengthened, not broken, by trauma and healing attempts.

With GORJULUI / Key no. 9, film director and visual artist Ștefan Constantinescu is tickling our imagination by using images with unexpected details and angles of the architecture of Gorjului metro station. Devoid of human presence (except one fleeting ghost-like appearance), cinematic to the core, the pictures push us towards wondering about the "what" and the "when" of what we are invited to witness: is this city asleep? Are we looking at relics of an extinct metropolis? The superimposition of a precise quote from the Noah's Ark–An Improbable Space Survival Kit, a book about the colonisation of outer space he is writing with scholar Corina Ilea, further complicates the reading of the intervention. GOLD / Key no. 32, his second intervention, is the last one in the series of three reprints. It is a step back in time to socialist Bucharest of the '60s, researched by the artists using propaganda pictures. The selected works from his An infinite blue are an extensive series of fascinatingly faithful drawings depicting the Bucharest of those times: folkloric celebrations, leisure activities in parks or state-owned restaurants and hotels, the hard work in state-of-the-art factories, etc.

In HANDLING HISTORIES / Key no. 10, artists Sabine Bitter & Helmut Weber divert the often-used comparison with Paris—romanticised under the phrase "Little Paris"—into fresh territory. Based on an impressive visual resemblance they unfold between two rather recent projects—the socialist housing project on Unirii Boulevard (the '80s), in the center of Bucharest, and the Abraxas housing complex at the outskirts of Paris (early '80s)—the contribution is a sharp case study of the recent geographies of globalisation.

By including more samples such as Sofia and Skopje from their large-scale collages, mashing icons of postmodern architecture from similar research series in the region (*Making Ruins, Boulevards, Banlieues and Other Samples of Decorated Histories*), Sabine & Helmut are building provocative connections, off the beaten paths.

INTERSECTIONS / Key no. 11, delivered by urbanist Gruia Bădescu, is a proper character study of Bucharest: multilayered, paradoxical, with references abounding and collage like imagery. A bundle of unconventional invisible threads with cities like Cairo, Beirut, Warsaw or places in Latin America are all called upon to highlight the (unparalleled) eclecticism of the Romanian capital. A typical, yet atypical post-socialist city with a cityscape infinitely fragmented. It seems that Bucharest can only be seen by overlapping an elevated perspective with a commitment to examining its roots.

JOURNEYS / Key no. 12 by writer, journalist and activist Ioana Ulmeanu, is a mesmerising look at the city through the widescreen windows of tram 16, one of the longest lines of public transport. Through her sharp eye, and the habit of making mental notes in a fictional diary during her almost daily trips to work, the texture of the city is vividly sketched. She scrutinises not only the road, but also her fellow travellers with an acute sense of curiosity and warmth. Many say riding a bus (or tram?) is a sad hobby, but if the promises of journeys with tram 16 are the ones outlined by Ioana Ulmeanu, we foresee it entering the list of informal off-the-beaten-track tours.

Bucharest, like all other capital cities, offends with the sins of being cold, crushing, unfriendly and hard to navigate. At least at first sight. So what are the tools a youngster can use to get closer to the heart of a city he is acquainted with? Under the title KINSHIP, Key no. 13 presents the glimpse of a method employed by artist Decebal Scriba in the early '70s after moving to the big city. Part of the pioneering generations studying design, Scriba decided to dissect the appearance of public space—public furniture, communications devices, information displays—as a way to break the city into pieces, to see its faults, to think of ways to improve it and eventually to come closer to it, even relearning to love it. These archival photographic impressions, now "reactivated", create a bi-directional arch in time, being both historically relevant for the dynamics between Bucharest and its inhabitants, and anticipatory for Scriba's subsequent practice as a conceptual artist and photographer.

What would be your method?

LAWNMOWER DYSPHORIA, Key no. 14, handled by musician and composer Sillyconductor, is an investigation into and a coming to terms with which realm proves to actually be the noisiest: the big city or the countryside villages. Setting up his ultimate acoustic head-to-head between the familiar—urban—soundscape and the more remote—natural—settings, Sillyconductor simultaneously becomes a sharp observer of the various transformations undergone by the latter. His surprising conclusions that the noises of the city are much more comforting, inspiring, nuanced and escapist is not speculative at all, but rather proved with meticulous measurements and rationale.

MEMORY / Key no. 15 offered by Andrei Dinu, is a concatenation of memories for what makes Bucharest an inspiring home for his work as edgy fashion label Prosper Center: upbeat settings, beaming frequencies of the underground creative scene, dazzling peculiarities that work as comfort food for thought. Images of his hybridised fashion design added in the mix—and, suddenly, the skin / surface of the city gains unexpected depth and texture.

NEOCLASSICAL / Key no. 16 by curator Geir Haraldseth, clashes two disparate anecdotes about chewing gum into a wondrous starting point for addressing his initial question: what is this city made of? Having the curiosity and the wit to discover details escaping most people, and also the distance to scrutinise the city without nostalgia or resentment, his intervention takes the shape of a refreshing critique of crumbling symbols, stemming from Bucharest's recent—megalomaniacal—past.

With O / Key no. 17, visual artist and performer Jimmy Robert is taking us on a trip to a possible future of the city. Unexpected, glossy, sleek, disquieting and spooky, his take on Bucharest is not entirely dystopian. Sultry sensations and illicit affairs leak through new realities to feed the concentrated drops of text to conjure up epiphanies hauntologists would be proud of.

Myth-making in flawless execution.

Key no. 18 / I'M TELLING YOU STORIES. TRUST ME is reprinted as homage to late artist Ioana Nemeș, co-founder of KILOBASE BUCHAREST. Originally commissioned by Idea magazine (2005), the conversation with Stuart Aarsman unveils several memorable snippets from her past as a sportswoman, her fascination with language and her hyper-subjective attempts of objectively understanding time. It also proved to be an early introduction into the thinking behind her major series Monthly Evaluations. The insert is fascinating in the context of this book also for the numerous minuscule details depicting places, real and fictional, in a Bucharest that was the backdrop—at times inspiring and tender and at others frustrating and haunting—of most of her life. Life and art are marching into each other thus rendering another form of self-evaluation: hijacking the interview as artistic medium.

In QUEER / Key no. 19, artist Karol Radziszewski revisits the experience of a trip in Bucharest, organised back in 2007, in order to research the queer scene for a special issue of the cult magazine DIK Fagazine, which was dedicated entirely to Romania. The intervention of the Polish artist is not a simple act of remembrance, but is built as a return to Bucharest in several moments—some happy and some painful as far as identity politics is concerned. It's an idiosyncratic mini-document to add to the archive of a time when queer Bucharest was definitely less in sight.

PERIPHERY / Key no. 20 looks as if artist Lea Rasovszky decided to twerk a possible national portrait gallery by championing a panoply of outcasts. Characters that the city of Bucharest might as well have been presenting to her over time, her subjects are drawn with a touch of magical realism and earnest affection. They are somehow familiar, full of life and resilience, yet distilling the turmoil of someone who was often labeled as being eccentric.

RESILIENCE / Key no. 21, a series of drawings made by visual artist Ștefan Botez works as a minimalist miniature fresco. Spread over seven pages, alongside a short melancholic decryption, it tells the story of a plant, Alianthus altissima (also known as the tree of heaven or ghetto palm), in different phases of development. A blue metaphor about the artistic life and the development in conditions, often not of the most favourable kind, in the urban landscape of a Bucharest that can swallow one without blinking.

The situation of stray dogs had for several decades been one of the most divisive topics in any conversation about Bucharest. With her STRAYING / Key no. 22 narrative, curator Simina Neagu takes a step back and in a gorgeous exercise of empathy and humility she is accompanying the ghost of her late dog, wise Mărgica, in an unlikely journey through Bucharest. Evoking both the joys and the miseries of life as stray dogs, listening carefully to the thoughtful argumentation of Mărgica, Simina can't but learn from such generous non-human perspectives. And so do we.

Key no. 23 titled TRESPASSING offers a fascinating scaffolding to study from different vantage points a massive phenomenon that had not been widely approached in academia before: the termopaneizare (double-glazification in English) of countless blocks and flats and houses in Bucharest. Anthropologist Bogdan Iancu slides between templates of cerebral analysis and firsthand examination, engaging field research to define new terms and reappraise the shifts in power relations between the city (or the state) and its citizens.

In UNCHARTED FOOTBALL EXPRESS / Key no. 24, anthropologist Andrei Mihail captures a somewhat forgotten process of transformation in the recent history of the city: the disappearance of an entire network of neighbourhood stadiums closely linked to a dense system of industrial infrastructure. At its peak, such a network of sport venues had an impact on the quality of life of hundreds of thousands of inhabitants. Unfolding in vivid details the stories of four stadiums that were part of the CFR (Romanian Railway Company) sport facilities, this contribution sharply mirrors both their gratifying past and derelict present. And reading between the lines the very reasons for their demise.

VIOLENT NATURE, the contribution of theatre director and performer Mihai Lukács, transforms the dramatic circumstances of an earthquake—a natural disaster deemed by specialists as inevitable for Bucharest—into a profound metaphor to set in motion major social transformations. Poetry at its most empathic construction, Key no. 25 unearths resources of empathy and latent solidarity in community structures sedated by capitalism.

Key no. 26 marks the return of performer and choreographer Mihai Mihalcea to his own name, after a decade of having performed under the moniker Farid Fairuz (who did an intervention in the initial KILOBASE BUCHAREST A–H book). In WETLANDS, Bucharest is dreamt of with feverish open eyes while being within the big, wet enclave of concrete that nature miraculously reclaimed, forming the Văcărești Delta. Oozing desire, linking bodily practices, spectacle and wilderness, his intervention claims the same wet enclave for all—queers or not—that feel displaced in the countless dry and dull blocks of flats that make up the city.

In the dead of night, Cosima Opârtan, performer, musician and muse, dives deep into the underworld of Bucharest, populated by outsiders and insiders, sensitivity and bravado, bodies moving in space and bodies moving on the generous spectrum of gender identity. An interlude between worlds, in a fractured joint, (CORP.) X / Key no. 27 brings to the surface crumbs from a vital scene for a city that wants to be diverse, open and alive.

As witnesses of those days, we are glad to now have enough distance from what life meant for most in '90s Bucharest: a wild and rather traumatic and draining process of transformation. Get ready to grab Key no. 28 by photographer Juergen Teller. Precise, raw and memorable—and an early example of his sharp eye and particular display of spontaneity—one can see the contribution YEAR 1990 as either a compelling, genuine flashback or a newly implanted memory.

When a lack of clear identity can work as a compliment, one needs the clarity and courage to take advantage. This is the thesis handed out by artist Hans Leonard Krupp in ZERO / Key no. 29, where the sense of possibilities for Bucharest seems endless. A zero point to restart afresh: spontaneous and life affirming.

Irina Bujor

ia an artist surviving the provincial life in Romania and Germany. Their work is based on formal associations which open a singular poetic vein; multilayered images and installations are highlighting the fragility and instability that question our seemingly certain reality.

By applying a wide variety of analytic strategies, Irina Bujor develops a multifaceted practice around ordinary phenomena that tend to go unnoticed in topics they are obsessed with: laughter, gender, factories producing popular culture and things permeating other things.

The work of Irina Bujor was exhibited at Simultan Festival, Timișoara (RO), A plus A gallery, Venice (IT), Kunsthal Gent (BE), Porous Space, Vienna (AT), *On Floating Grounds. Ways of Practicing Imponderability* exhibition in the frame of Art Encounters Biennial 1st Edition, Timișoara (RO), Galeria Anca Poterașu, Bucharest (RO), Penthouse Art Residency (NH Brussels Bloom x Harlan Levey Projects), Brussels (BE), photo_graz 014. Biennale der steirischen Fotokunst. Kunstfreiraum Papierfabrik, Graz (AT), Narrenkastl, Frohnleiten (AT), Kulturkontakt, Vienna (AT).

They contributed to collective projects like *Managing Structural Bird Problems* - Die Philosophischen Bauern, Kabinett, Akademie Schloß Solitude, Stuttgart (DE) and *KILOBASE BUCHAREST A – H*, Museion Bolzano (IT).

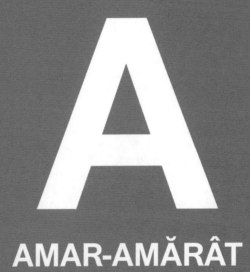

A

AMAR-AMĂRÂT

7.

Way back I borrowed from a friend a book titled Sad by Design by Geert Lovink. When it comes to reading, I don't have any patterns, rather I'm into chance encounters with disparate thoughts. For some unknown reasons Sad by Design didn't make it to the top of the pile from which every now and then I extract something to read. Therefore, I don't know yet what the book was about, but I kept seeing the title and it always bothered me.

Months after the world was altered into a never-ending nightmare, I suddenly found myself in a desperate need to powder sadness and the avalanche of terrible news for a less dreadful look. Stranded at home, like all the others privileged enough to have a home and a job that can be done remotely, I started unearthing boxes of memories and miscellaneous things; among which I found a wooden horse marionette almost entirely covered in intricate mirror fragments. An indecisive object between a semi-functional ethnic souvenir and a toy from a queer puppet theater.

The state of my discovery is far from perfect. The coarse tail looks decimated, or maybe it's just testament to the worst grooming treatment a toy can get. There is something wrong with the strings moving the limbs. The painting was erased brutally on one side of the face, while the other side shows a weird grin rather than a smile.

Yet, it made my day.

It made me smile by reflecting the sun in dancing flashes of light, by moving sillily and always falling to the left while I was trying to maneuver it.

I got the horse maybe three years ago in Bucharest at CIRCA 1703- 3071, an oversized treasure chest and store of vintage design run by Laura Paraschiv. Among many categories of objects on display, from design icons to upcycled oldies and happy objects, one category is never for sale: the priceless Amar-Amărât.

I recall her exuberant laughter while saying: "this is an Amar-Amărât."

An approximate English translation would be The Bittered-Bitter, The Saddened-Sad, The Pitiful-Miserable. Without intention, Laura formulated, and later spread around, the most audacious panegyric of bittersweetness by assigning Amar-Amărât to a set of objects that would never fit in the definitions of beauty. Fallouts from the heaven of perfect production, always carrying something charmingly wrong in design, every Amar-Amărât at CIRCA 1703 – 3071 is something close to a tiny miracle, an artifact sad and utterly hilarious and cheerful at the same time.

An awkward portrait of a dog with an eye defect qualifies for this category as well as a ceramic rendition of a polar bear with eccentric proportions. It can be a painting of a child looking freaky, menacing and silly or a glass owl with a clumsy sticker as a face. Or it can be something with glimpses of unorthodoxy or political incorrectness.

While many wondered at those objects, Laura stood strong with her decision not to sell. Heaven knows how much I begged her. Finally she would give me the horse as a gift, refusing to sell it.

Times changed in the last few months.
Radically.

We will need more of these Amar-
Amărât objects, inherently peculiar and able to
play a comedy for us, both heartbreaking and
heartwarming.
Amusing ourselves to survival.

/ \/ .

Bucharest has changed too since I left half a decade ago.
Not so radically though.

If I ever see it as my city again, I will not let it split me in two (like the first time I moved there).

At home.
Departed from the realities around, in the darkroom of an ugly, overpriced apartment I rented, I tried to be myself: a they sun dancing in synch with funny shadows of my fingers, enjoying overwhelming waves of hyper-sensory stimulation of hanging around in imaginary places, leather catsuits, wet dreams of lenticular bras. Planningtorock, She Diamond, Against Me!, Sophie, Ah-Mer-Ah-Su, San Cha, Anohni all together with me.

Outside home.
Departed from my inner reality, careful to construct an artificial shield as a provincial, geeky little bird. Running for cover in a city feeding daily my fears, spirit deformed as it proved better to lie: I'm just like you.

Myself and my queer sisters in Bucharest will need more of these Amar-Amărât objects, inherently peculiar and able to play a comedy for us, both heartbreaking and heartwarming. Amusing ourselves to survival.

I/ .

*As One who knows something of the hard-
to-pin-down science of spotting objects that
make us laugh, that stir us awake, Laura, my
friend, you should share more of your bunch
of Amar-Amărât.*

*You should dedicate yourself to scouting for
them full-time, both close and afar.*
Organizing a store just for them.
Or an improvised museum.
*Or a social institution of sorts; for a serendipi-
tous proliferation of Amar-Amărât.*
Amusing ourselves to survival.

Serioja Bocsok

is an artist, photographer and graphic designer working in Bucharest, Romania. He studied Photography and Video at the University of Arts in Bucharest and currently he is enrolled in a MA in Visual Anthropology at the National School of Political and Administrative Studies, Bucharest.

Serioja Bocsok is working primarily with photography, exploring how political and power structures change both the appearance and meaning of landscapes and the built and inhabited environment.

Oftentimes he delves into photographic archives and vernacular photography as a strategy for artistic research, but also with the aim to develop new works revolving around processes of image-making and construction of memory.

The works of Serioja Bocsok were presented in exhibitions like *On Floating Grounds. Ways of Practicing Imponderability*, Art Encounters, Timișoara (RO), curated by Ioana Mandeal, *What About Poor Gregor Samsa?*, Anca Poterașu Gallery, Bucharest (RO), curated by Ioana Mandeal, *WHAT ABOUT Y[OUR] MEMORY*, MNAC Bucharest (RO) curated by Irina Cios & Iosif Király etc.

🌐 https://seriojabocsok.com

BUZEȘTI

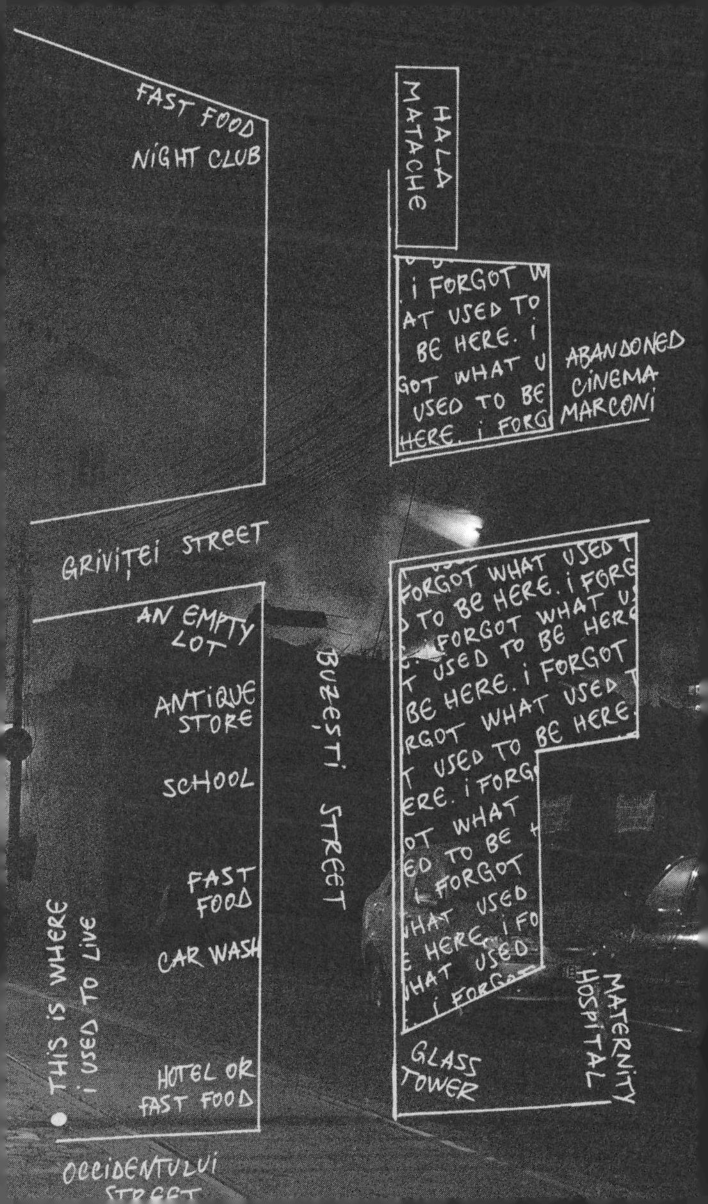

FAST FOOD

NIGHT CLUB

HALA MATACHE

i FORGOT W
AT USED TO
BE HERE. i
GOT WHAT U
USED TO BE
HERE. i FORG

ABANDONED
CINEMA
MARCONI

GRIVIȚEI STREET

AN EMPTY
LOT

ANTIQUE
STORE

SCHOOL

FAST
FOOD

CAR WASH

BUZEȘTI STREET

FORGOT WHAT USED T
TO BE HERE. i FORG
FORGOT WHAT U
T USED TO BE HERE
BE HERE. i FORGOT
RGOT WHAT USED
T USED TO BE HERE.
ERE. i FORG
OT WHAT
ED TO BE
i FORGOT
HAT USED
HERE. i FO
HAT USED
i FORG

MATERNITY
HOSPITAL

THIS IS WHERE
i USED TO LIVE

HOTEL OR
FAST FOOD

GLASS
TOWER

OCCIDENTULUI
STREET

On 23rd of November 2010, I heard on the news that authorities were planning to demolish in haste, during the night, some of the historical buildings on Buzești Street, a place close to my home at that time. I instantly decided to go there and take photos, although, to be honest, I didn't have much interest in a photojournalistic approach, nor was I very aware of the meaning of such a gesture. I only wanted to document what was happening in front of me, although I remember having an acute feeling that some kind of injustice was being brought upon the whole Buzești neighbourhood.

*

Many years later, more precisely this spring, I participated in an online course about urbanism, during which we discussed, specifically, the case of the demolitions on Buzești Street. It made me plunge abruptly back into one of those cold nights in late November 2010. Not long after the course, I was suddenly struck by something: a feeling I wasn't prepared for, nor had felt before—I couldn't remember how Buzești Street used to look like.

I couldn't remember the buildings, even though I was staring at the images I once made during one of the nights when the actual demolition was happening. I couldn't remember how wide the street was, surely not as wide as the corporate desert it's slowly turned into since. I couldn't remember where shops were, which buildings were there, which of them were empty or abandoned, except for the old cinema.

A decade has passed since the area was torn down, and one would not be mistaken to say that the promises of new and shiny were never fulfilled on Buzești Street. There is only one new building on the right side, an enormous glass tower, replacing the dense urban tissue which was once built there. On the left side, the remaining old buildings are still there, some abandoned, looking worse every year. Another structure appeared, where there used to be an empty lot, at the corner with Griviței Street. I think it's still unused to this day.

*

Nonetheless, cool specialty coffee shops started to sprout. The eco-bio-corporate restaurants came too, packaging themselves as co-ops. This new, beautiful, clean world emerged as a cosmeticised facade of the crumbling old quarter, begging to be photographed, tagged, posted, tweeted, grammed. It's not even about consuming anymore, but about creating kinds of memories. Only to let them soon disappear, to be forgotten.

*

Walking in between worlds on Buzești Street, it turns out to be, actually, quite frustrating for me not to remember how parts of Bucharest used to look like. I've called the capital my home since 2009, but it feels like I've somehow been living in different cities. Or in two different timelines.

studioBASAR

is both an architecture studio and a spatial practice for the production of public and community space founded in 2006 by Alex Axinte and Cristi Borcan in Bucharest, Romania. Through research by design, place-making, co-design, co-production and civic pedagogy, studioBASAR constructs intermediary formats and builds spaces which enable collaboration processes and foster users' participation towards a more accessible and just city. The work of the studio includes over the past years the design of the Romanian Pavilion at the Venice Art Biennale, 2009 (IT), the publication of *Evicting the Ghost. Architectures of Survival*, P+4 Publications (eds.) 2010, the development of pop-up installation *Public Bath*, 2014, Bucharest (RO), the collaborations with civic groups developing "Tei Community Centre", 2016, Bucharest (RO), the building of interdisciplinary live educational program "City School", 2015-2017, Bucharest (RO), or the participation at The Chicago Architecture Biennial, 2019, Chicago (US).

Alex Axinte is an architect, living and working in Bucharest. Currently Alex is a PhD student at the University of Sheffield, Sheffield School of Architecture (SSoA), working as an independent researcher from an intermediary position between applied research, engaged education, participatory design and civic activation.

Cristi Borcan is a Bucharest based architect, a teaching assistant at the UAUIM Architecture University and co-author of civic, community, educational and cultural projects. His research is currently focused on collective modes of producing social spaces and spatial practices of commoning.

🌐 http://studiobasar.ro

COMMONS

TEI COMMUNITY CENTER
Bucharest, 2016

Lacul Tei Civic Initiative Group (GICLT) is one of the informal groups of citizens that emerged in Bucharest in the last ten years. It's part of a larger movement of civic engagement and activism where neighbours started to coalesce, reacting to the authorities' management of the common resources of the city. Supported by NGOs specialised in community organisation like The Resource Center for Public Participation (CeRe), these groups slowly became critical actors in Bucharest's civic life.

In October 2016, GICLT initiated a community space in their neighbourhood as a collaboration between active citizens, architects and community organisers. Placed in the local park, Tei Community Center is the spatial answer to the lack of the neighbourhood's spaces for cultural dissemination, educational production and community interaction. A space for "meeting people and doing things in common" was one of the needs identified by members of the group among the community.

The center hosts events organised by the group and by different NGOs, in line with its civic-community and cultural-educational directions. Housed in a transformed shipping container, the center functions as a catalyst for the group's actions and activities, and acts as a shared resource managed by social practices of commoning (Bollier, 2016).[1] These collaborative and co-produced activities facilitated a set of spatial relations among citizens that continuously enacts and reproduces a common space.

Team: Alex Axinte, Cristi Borcan, Matei David (studioBASAR)/ Elena Anghel, Vivi Cernescu, Silvia Cruceanu, Roberto Pătrășcoiu, Ioana Maria Rusu, Irina Sandu (GICLT)/ Vlad Cătună (CeRe). Tei Community Center is a partnership between GICLT, studioBASAR and CeRe, and was funded through the *Urbaniada* competition.
1   Bollier, D., *Commoning as a Transformative Social Paradigm,* 2016. Available from: https://thenextsystem.org/ [Accessed on 11.09.2020].

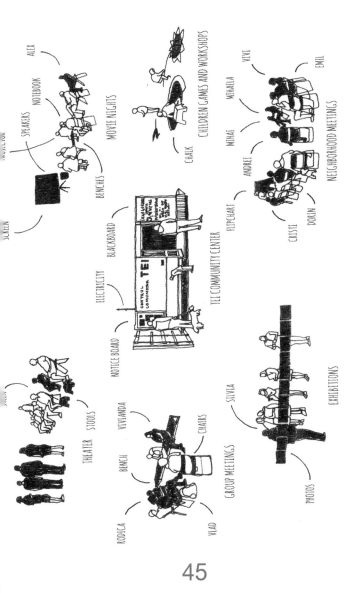

45

CITY SCHOOL (CS)
Bucharest, 2015-2017

In the context of a bottom-up civic revival of the urban communities, the dominant educational paradigm for urban professionals in Romania is still heavily based on disciplinary bounded methods, tailored for abstract users.

Following a series of public space workshops[1], the CS project aimed to reclaim the University's civic role. Designed as an alternative, independent and interdisciplinary project, CS piloted a situated version of an engaged education process. Students and tutors from architecture, sociology and landscape design worked together with local stakeholders. And so it was that the Bucharest Metropolitan Library (BMB) became the CS case study, partner and host. By involving diverse actors, like universities, neighbours and public administration, the CS participants co-designed with the local partners the transformation of the interiors of two public libraries and their exterior spaces.

CS actions triggered the users' participation while enabling a mutual learning that was mediated by the world (Freire, 2017).[2] CS created a safe intermediary space, facilitating the co-production of knowledge in support of the commoning process and as a common resource in itself.

46

Tutors: Alex Axinte, Cristi Borcan, Tudor Elian, Bogdan Iancu, Daniela Calciu, Anca Crețu, Diana Culescu, Ana-Dora Matei, Andrei Tudor Mihail, Alecs Vasiliu. "City School" was a project coordinated by studioBASAR and financed through the *Mobilizing Excellency Program*, developed by Bucharest Community Foundation.
1   Place-making workshops coordinated by studioBASAR since 2011 in cities across Romania, Republic of Moldova, Czech Republic and Germany.
2   Freire, P., *Pedagogy of the Oppressed*. UK, Penguin Random House, 2017.

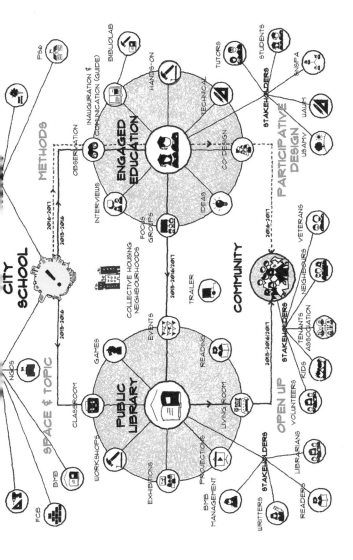

THE TRAILER FOR RESEARCH AND ACTIVATION
Bucharest, 2016

Bucharest's public spaces have undergone a process of radical privatisation and commodification. Powerful actors exploit the public space as a resource for either profit or votes. Local actors, such as cultural, educational or civic initiatives, are lacking the spatial tools for the production of public and community spaces.

With this background, the Trailer was designed as a tool for place-making to be shared free of charge among different organisations. Built on a light transport vehicle, the Trailer opens by extending its metal structure and flapping down its wooden boards. It quickly adapts to the local geography and its operators' needs and pops out into workshop tables, a bar and a cooking table, exhibition boards, bookshelves, a small stage and an outdoor cinema. Since 2016 the Trailer was used in more than forty events by the Bucharest Metropolitan Library network, several civic groups and cultural NGOs.

Acting as a piece of mobile architecture, the Trailer skilled up its operators and empowered their organisations to reach out to communities deprived of access to valuable and meaningful public spaces. The Trailer performed as a relational device among different groups, creating an ad-hoc space for practice and learning, for sharing skills and knowledge, becoming a situated form of temporary urban commons.

48

Team: Alex Axinte, Cristi Borcan, Matei David, Tudor Elian.
"The Trailer for Research and Activation" is a "City School" associated project, coordinated by studioBASAR and financed through the *Mobilizing Excellency Program*, developed by Bucharest Community Foundation.

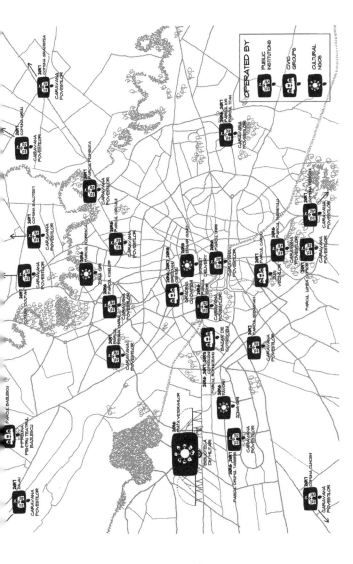

SPACES OF (LATENT) COMMONING
Alex Axinte

Thriving neoliberal policies, fuelled by a hegemonic anti-communist narrative, have brought major changes to Romania's cities in the past thirty years. Hosting most of its urban population, collective housing neighbourhoods are facing radical privatisation, collapsing public infrastructure and rampant individualisation. However, nested by surviving socialist infrastructures, a range of appropriation practices, emergent civic institutions and everyday protocols of collaboration are evidencing what De Angelis (2017) calls "latent commons".[1]

These estates' foundational modernist project still instigate some instances of commoning. From transforming the leftover green areas into shared gardens, to the collective use of the public infrastructure or the spatialised care for animals; while constantly repairing, reusing and transforming the in-between spaces into places of interaction, the inhabitants are acting as (latent) commoners. They are weaving an implicit, discrete and anonymous network of a distinct relational practice among people, spaces, plants and animals.

From the position of an engaged practitioner I'm seeking to bring research-based evidence in supporting the emergent spaces of commoning. By articulating a version of urban commons situated in the ex-socialist city, the ongoing research builds up as an alternative narrative. This research aims to value these practices in the context of radical privatisation of public resources and ecological crises and seeks to work as a model for a scaled up reclamation of the civic commons.

1   De Angelis, M., *Omnia Sunt Communia. On the Commons and the Transformation to Postcapitalism*, London, Zed Books, 2017.

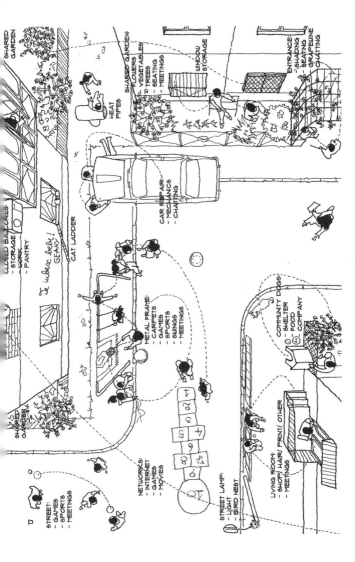

THE NEIGHBOURHOOD AS COMMONS
Cristi Borcan

What makes a community in a city that went through dramatic social and spatial transformations during the last fifty-sixty years? What does it mean to "be-in-common" in a society that mistrusts authorities, disbelieves in collective actions and generates individualistic behaviours? What are the spaces that could help redefine and rebuild a community?

Some possible answers can be found in the forms of active citizenship performed by the civic groups in Bucharest and their multiple, diverse and real claims on public space. Kiseleff Civic Initiative Group is one such group that I'm a member of and that's been active in the 1 Mai/Kiseleff neighbourhood in Bucharest since 2017. Through different spatial actions, events and initiatives organised around the neighbourhood the group emphasised the contextual and relational dimension of living together in the city.

The members of the group are maybe best described as agents of care[1] for the neighbourhood's common resources. Central to their actions is the belief that the city is a shared resource open to all citizens. By acting against the continuous enclosures, aggressive privatisations and the extreme commodification and commercialisation of these resources, and voicing concerns for the ways the city is managed, they claim access to urban spaces and their right to participate in the production of the city and the shaping of their living space.

The spatial relations performed collectively by acting in the public space of the neighbourhood produces a situated community of practice; a community that practices the neighbourhood as commons.

1   Fitz, A., Krasny, E., (eds.), *Critical Care. Architecture and Urbanism for a Broken Planet,* Vienna, Architekturzentrum Wien and Cambridge, MA, MIT Press, 2019.

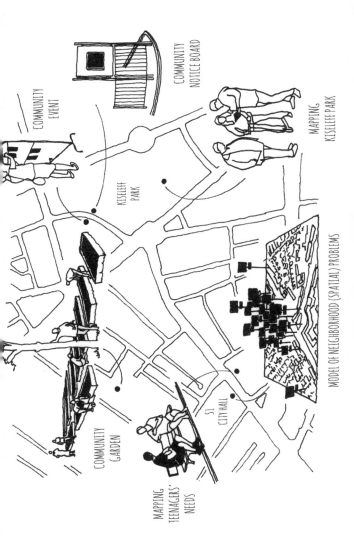

COMMUNITY EVENT

COMMUNITY NOTICE BOARD

MAPPING KISELEFF PARK

KISELEFF PARK

COMMUNITY GARDEN

MAPPING TEENAGERS' NEEDS

S1 CITY HALL

MODEL OF NEIGHBORHOOD (SPATIAL) PROBLEMS

53

Iuliana Dumitru

b. 1985 in 2 Mai village, Romania. She graduated the Faculty of Sociology in 2008, and the MA program at the Center of Excellence in Image Studies (CESI, University of Bucharest) in 2011. Still at CESI she is currently writing an interdisciplinary PhD about narrative cartographies of 2 Mai and Vama Veche, two villages from the seaside, important for the Romanian artists' community before 1989 and after. Based on her doctoral research, she curated *From Near to Far. Visual Cartographies of the Spaces 2 Mai and Vama Veche* exhibition at The National Museum of the Romanian Peasant, Bucharest (RO).

Numerous encounters with art and artists happened over the years in projects like: *Pandora—Art & Electronics* at the Faculty of Electronics Telecommunications and Information Technology (2015-2017), the revitalisation of the Costa-Foru house (2015), conducting interviews for Zeppelin Association—part of the exhibitions *Bucharest-South* (2015) or doing research for the Romanian Cultural Institute project "X:20 Romanian Art after 1989" (2011-2012).

Starting with January 2017 she is assistant curator for tranzit.ro/Bucharest (member of Tranzit Network, tranzit.org) where she was involved in organizing different exhibitions, like: *The Veil of Peace* (2017), Yuri's Leiderman *Self-portrait with Valerian* (2017), *Shadoof* by Kiki Mihuță (2017). In 2019, she co-curated alongside with Raluca Voinea the group exhibition *Artistic Research of the Plants*.

Iuliana Dumitru is contributing to the international project Collection Collective starting with 2018 and she is a member of CORNER Football+Society editorial team since 2017.

🌐 https://corner.ro

Ștefan Ghenciulescu

PhD, is an architect, curator and critic. He is the editor-in-chief of Zeppelin, a leading magazine of architecture and urban culture unfolding both in print (bookazine four times a year) and online. Co-founded together with Cosmina Goagea and Constantin Goagea in the early 2000s, Zeppelin is producing besides the magazine a range of thought-provoking exhibitions, conferences, research projects, books and urban interventions.

Several of the books, exhibitions and research projects he wrote, co-curated and co-edited, focus on Bucharest: the city where Ștefan was born, where he lives and works, a city he both loves and despises.

His main research areas are contemporary architecture and the city, historical modernity, public space and the commons, and, broadly, any crossover between architecture and human studies, activism, art, etc.

His architectural practice focuses mainly on the transformation of existing buildings, exhibition design, interventions in public space.

Ștefan also teaches at the "Ion Mincu" University of Architecture and Urbanism, Bucharest (RO). He was a visiting professor at several European architecture schools, more recently the Vienna University of Technology (AT), UCL Louvain – LOCI, Brussels (BE).

Awards for the Zeppelin team include: finalists at the European Public Space of the Year 2011, several prizes and nominations within national architecture exhibitions, the Romanian pavilion for the 2006 Venice Architecture Biennale.

⊕ https://e-zeppelin.ro

KILOBASE BUCHAREST

The duo was initiated by Dragoș Olea in 2010 together with Ioana Nemeș (1979-2011) as an artistic project that took the form of a nomadic art space. Gradually, KILOBASE BUCHAREST became a hybrid between curatorial project and nomadic gallery.

Since 2016, KILOBASE BUCHAREST is conceptualised by Dragoș Olea and curator Sandra Demetrescu.

KILOBASE BUCHAREST explores three main topics: economy, queer and Bucharest, drawing consistently from the local context. KILOBASE BUCHAREST also investigates the depths, intensities and micropolitics of experimental collaboration practices involving artists.

KILOBASE BUCHAREST curated, exhibited, produced works or exhibitions at Kulturkontakt, Vienna (AT), Oberwelt, Stuttgart (DE), Museion, Bolzano (IT), Eastside Projects, Birmingham (UK), Viennafair, Vienna (AT), Brukenthal Museum of Contemporary Art, Sibiu (RO), CCN, Graz (AT), Eastwards Prospectus, Bucharest (RO), Supersymmetrica, Madrid (ES), etc.

⊕ http://kilobasebucharest.ro

DAYDREAMS

ONE THING TO WISH FROM/ FOR BUCHAREST
Iuliana Dumitru

I grew up in a small village by the seaside that was crowded in the summer but empty the rest of the year, and since I was fifteen years old my dream was to move to Bucharest. From far away the city had this wonderful glow—with all its museums, cinemas and clubs. It offered so many possibilities like good schools, better prepared teachers and libraries.

At twenty I moved there to go to University and finally my love story with the city began. It has its ups and downs like any other love story, but the city made room for me: Bucharest offered me a place where I found and improved myself. I found places that I can call my second home, tranzit.ro/București being one of them, and I have friends in almost all neighbourhoods except Pantelimon.[1] There is a peculiar mix of planning, privatisation and guerrilla take over of common space which I sometimes enjoy it as it gives the city a certain vibe, and gives you the exact freedom you need to plant a pine tree in front of your apartment building.

A few years ago I was part of a project, "Actopolis – Bucharest-South", where we asked people from the south part of Bucharest to be mayors for ten minutes. We had designed a pavilion where there was the mayoral office; we had a desk, flowers, a stamp, an oath and lots of papers to fill in. One of the sheets asked them to imagine the future city of Bucharest South.

1   Pantelimon is one of Bucharest's most known neighbourhoods because of a Romanian rap group—B.U.G. MAFIA and it became well known at the beggining of the '90s. The band members, who grew up in the area, were singing about the harsh life of the people living there, about poverty and substance abuse. At fifteen years old I was a fan of the band and hoped that someday I would know someone from that neighborhood, but I never did.

As we liked to play with the idea of a future city, my partner and I developed this megalomaniacal futuristic and smart amusement park that you could connect to with your phone and have tailored-made experiences. But in reality the people who decided to play along and become mayors wished for grounded things, things like more buses with a time schedule, good infrastructure, safe hospitals, more parks, nothing utopic, nothing from the science fiction movies, as I'd thought they would. It was the moment when I realised that before dreams can start, the basics things need to work.

Understanding this in relation to the Bucharest art world I would say that we need good spaces, on the ground, spaces that do not collapse on you, spaces that last more than a season or two. Funding is really needed as well, in other words stability is what we want and need. But in my opinion, most of all, I think we need healthy human relationships, real conversations, honest talks, where we know more about what is behind someone's interests, why they are doing research, what keeps them going.

I feel that human relationships are the DNA of every good project that can happen. Now I see the city as an organism, a sick body, with only a few working organs that do their job but nothing more. For this body to survive and thrive, the organs need to start working together, to go a little bit further than, 'This is my job, it starts here and ends here.' We need to think and work like a whole. As I'm a social researcher, my favourite thing to do is ask other people what they think. So I've asked some friends, from different fields, what's their One Thing to Wish from/for Bucharest, so here are some answers:

Cristina (33), PR — 'Screaming phone booths, a white box where you can go inside and scream without anybody hearing you. Walking arm-in-arm hour, every day from Unirii Square to Romană Square people can walk holding arms. Another way to connect to people.'

Viorica (67), retired chemist — 'To fill the holes from the roads with flowers, then we will have meadows instead of roads.'

Eugen (33), philosopher — 'This city in a basic way is like a house without foundations. I can only think of practical stuff: subway from the airport, subway for all the neighbourhoods, something to mirror the identity of the city.'

Miruna (39), travel blogger — 'I would like for Bucharest to be surrounded by forest, once again, how Codrii Vlăsiei used to be. More green in the city and of course more bikes.'

Marian (37), energetic healer — 'More colour in the city and works of art with a positive message. Most of all artists should try to wake the consciousness in others and send good vibes through their art. And of course people to stop using their car horns.'

Rucsandra (42), writer

'Bucharest–like most of the big cities–is a place where most people live at the surface not knowing the history of the city, not knowing their neighbours or not even knowing the other parts of the city. I dream of a Bucharest where people regain their sense of belonging and reclaim their power to change things.'

'Bucharest is a beast that needs to be tamed through arts, through civic engagement, through research and through love.'

Matei (19), art student

'I would like to wish the city to forgive us, because we could do much more for it but we are crooks. We don't leave our comfort zones and we find excuses not to make a better society. Admitting and acknowledging our mistakes can be the first step to making it better and trying to solve its problems.'

CITY OF WITCHES AND WISHES
Ștefan Ghenciulescu

After living my life, working in and researching Bucharest, I can state with reasonable conviction that this absurd city mainly exists because of witchcraft. It survives and functions despite all apparent logic thanks to some sort of shabby yet energetic, half-reliable, seemingly absurd but oh so cunning magic.

Look, for instance, at its place of founding. There is no significant topography, no sea or lake, the river is not much to talk about, the old crossing of commercial roads just one among many in the area. There must have been some mysterious reason and maybe a neverending spell to make people believe in its existence and future.

More importantly, like all good magical places, it exists somewhere behind reality, or better said, it hides behind (and sometimes wraps and slides around) itself. Everywhere you are on a big and noisy boulevard, you turn a corner—any corner— and you find yourself thrown in a completely different realm—quiet villages, green yet with a strange mixture of higher, lower, older and very new buildings. Just across a bright office building lies a peasant house. Poor families live above luxury bars.

Bucharest does have a center and a periphery. But then, the center contains its own peripheries. Like some impossible geometric object, the center and the margins are everywhere. Slipping between worlds is the easiest thing to do—escaping the labyrinth of crooked streets maybe less so.

Everywhere in these strange villages you find strange houses: you can spot their Western inspiration—French Classicism, Modernism or Art Deco for instance, but then their scale and their profusion of ornaments don't match. One-storey homes bear as much decorations as a large French mansion. They are not set in stone, but rather poured from all kind of surrogates. Each of them lies alone among trees, and yet extremely close to its neighbour, they coagulate into armies of derelict but rather gentle gingerbread houses, rows of tales waiting to happen again.

Streets are for circulation and competition only: real public life, meaning the voluntary coming-together of people happens in gardens: public or private, a protected outside that is almost an inside. Going out to a café usually means going into a small fenced forest.

Speaking about greenery, it's both fascinating and disturbing the way plants, happily massacred since the formation of the city, manage to survive in cracks and holes and even to fight back. Sidewalks in Bucharest are a hilly landscape not just because of bad work and materials, corruption and neglect, but also because the roots push up. Quite often, older and newer walls are also bent and topped over by trees, mightier than concrete and steel. It seems that the bygone forest is somehow still present. It invades and cracks open the present and visible reality.

Magic here is rather approximate, fuzzy, patched up. No elves and fairies here, no crystalline perfection and clear and crisp architecture. Bucharest is rather like a witch's cottage on a metropolitan scale: in gingerbread or in bricks and concrete, but never finished, never pure. Bricolage is stronger than anything here, and it produces ever changing landscapes, where courtyards and houses melt into each other: everything is reworked incessantly. So are the rules. Smart or (usually) stupid and absurd, they are all happily bent and twisted.

That is not to say that, as in any tale worth its name, we lack conflict. Oh no, actually everybody fights everybody else. Sometimes, because the camps are diffuse, we are not even conscious that we're part of one. Nothing is completely good or bad, either, and the roles are not always clearly visible. For instance, the mad passion people feel here for their cars may well be the result of a collective love potion. The absurd amount of cars that are permanently trapped in traffic jams are maybe just instruments for producing exhaust fumes—terrible ingredients for a gigantic brew with an uncertain purpose. Obviously, not just the trees but also the cars have their magicians.

Sometimes, evil is clearer, as was the case of the war The Great and Bad Wizard Nicolae Ceaușescu (ostensibly, the President and Chairman of the Party) waged in the late '70s and in the '80s against Bucharest and its people. He didn't completely prevail, a lot of the city is still here. But, in a kind of perverse happy end, his monstrous Castle and evil new city seem poised to be loved happily ever after by the people they were forced upon. On the other hand, they've also changed, adapted, perverted, like everything else before and after them.

Now, thirty years after Ceaușescu's demise, there only seem to remain a lot of smaller wizards and their followers. We are all arguing, competing and trying to assert ourselves. And, like an enormously inflated version of *The Three Wishes*, the sum of all of our egotistical good wishes shapes a collective nightmare. Time maybe to weave some spells together, to build up a collective tale.

3 WISHES
Kilobase Bucharest

1   A city full of blocks, cars, Mega Image supermarkets, banks and pharmacies, yet paradoxically and painfully empty.

When it comes to progressive ideas—Universal Basic Income, anything transgressive about gender, tackling painful histories of Roma slavery or the deep gray areas where the state is withdrawing from responsibility of its acts—the exhausting, suffocating Bucharest turns into an almost[1] empty field.

One that is also crepuscular, subdued and isolated.

WHAT ABOUT TO WISH FOR EACH AND EVERY CITIZEN OF BUCHAREST TO RECEIVE THE EMPOWERING HUG OF PROGRESSIVE IDEAS?

A long, firm, warm, multiplied, addictive, altering embrace that should be.

1   As exceptions we could mention *Manifesto for the Gynecene* by Alexandra Pirici and Raluca Voinea, Giuvlipen Roma feminist theater company, Common Front for Housing Rights, Macaz cooperative, Triumf Amiria.

2 Anyone who has used public transport in Bucharest, went to pay taxes, or to a hospital knows how design is most of the time relegated to the corner as an outcast.

The terrible posters and prints, the lack of transparency in visual communication and ergonomics are many times forgotten.
Anything goes.

The shapes and ways images and words are circulating in these places is sometimes damaging. But more damaging is to realise that the disregard toward design is in fact a crass lack of care, of empathy.

WHAT ABOUT ENACTING A FANTASY: A SQUAD OF DESIGNERS TAKING OVER THE BUCHAREST CITY HALL OR SOME VITAL DEPARTMENTS THERE?

TO ENCIRCLE WITH CLINICAL PRECISION ALL DESIGN / VISUAL COMMUNICATION NEEDS OF STATE RUN PROVIDERS OF PUBLIC SERVICES: SCHOOLS, HOSPITALS, CITY HALLS, FISCAL AGENCIES, POLICE, SOCIAL ORGANISATIONS, PARKS ADMINISTRATIONS, ETC.
TO THINK, RETHINK AND REMODEL THE USE OF DESIGN IN THIS CITY.
TO TURN IT INTO AN ULTIMATE FORM OF USEFULNESS AND CARE.

3   But then, design of everything public being sharp
and clear and sober would be impossible here.

It would be Confusing.
It would feel Alien.
Maybe it would even feel stripped of cultural
meaning for the locals.

WOULDN'T IT BE A DREAM WORTH
TRYING—TO DIG, SCAN, ABSORB, HARVEST
AND FIND PLEASURE IN FLICKERS OF
ANYTHING TRANSGRESSIVE IN THE LOCAL
GREGARIOUSNESS OF KITSCH?

Sentimental, juicy, compelling, ballsy and vaginal,
the language of Bucharest vernacular/ kitsch to
be used for all of the above communication.

Apparatus 22

is a transdisciplinary art collective founded in January 2011 by Erika Olea, Maria Farcaș, Dragoș Olea together with Ioana Nemeș (1979-2011) in Bucharest, Romania. Since 2015 they have been working between Bucharest, Brussels and the Suprainfinit utopian realm.

They see themselves as a collective of daydreamers, citizens of many realms, researchers, poetic activists and (failed) futurologists interested in exploring the intricate relationships between economy, politics, gender studies, social movements, religion and fashion in order to understand contemporary society. A major topic of research and reflection in their practice is Suprainfinit universe: a world-making attempt to use hope critically in navigating present and future.

The work of Apparatus 22 was presented at La Biennale di Venezia 2013 (IT), MUMOK, Vienna (AT), BOZAR, Brussels (BE), MUSEION, Bolzano (IT), Kunsthalle Wien (AT), Académie Royale des Beaux-Arts de Bruxelles (BE), Akademie Schloss Solitude, Stuttgart (DE), MNAC, Bucharest (RO), KunstMuseum Linz (AT), La Triennale di Milano (IT), Trafó, Budapest (HU), Futura, Prague (CZ), Ujazdowski Castle, Warsaw (PL), TIME MACHINE BIENNIAL, Konji (BIH), Osage Foundation (HK), Progetto Diogene, Turin (IT), Closer Art Centre, Kiev (UA), CIAP, Hasselt (BE), Suprainfinit Gallery, Bucharest (RO), GALLLERIAPIÙ, Bologna (IT), Survival Kit 11, LCCA Riga (LV), Autostrada Bienniale Prizren (XK); performances at MAK, Vienna (AT), Steirischer Herbst, Graz (AT), Stedelijk Museum & De Appel CP, Amsterdam (NL), Kunsthal Gent (BE), Yarat Academy, Baku (AZ), Württembergischer Kunstverein Stuttgart (DE), Drodesera Festival, Dro (IT), SMAK Gent (BE), etc.

EUROPA
~ ON ~
MAGIC

A microcosmos of cheap
Made in China stuff

A paradise of organised crim

It used to cover around
eight hectares

*Those who dig the mountains
of cheap will be the ones
who'll find a fake diamond.*

EUROPA
INFAMOUS WHOLESALE
COMPLEX

On the outskirts of Bucharest

From the early 90s till 2019

- It caught fire a few times during the silent wars between various groups of interests

- Feverish business transactions would happen between 2 - 5 a.m.

- A prototype for wholesale centres in Romania

- In its heyday it housed close to 5,000 stalls

- *Fake and real - abundant, perplexing*

Shelter for an impressive community of Chinese, Vietnamese, Arab and Romanian businesses thriving on tax evasion

Cheap escapism in a parallel reality, always hardcore, cute & kitsch

Authorities estimated that tax evasion in the complex amounted to more than € 300 million a year

Mood – hysterical, atmosphere – dystopian, display – flamboyant

RIDDLE NO. 101

A shiny Kingdom of
Pretty (knockoffs),
Monaco lurking (in shadows);
An epic Silk Road, entangled,
only in wee hours.
A shady ecosystem
(upon periphery)
to glitch Bucharest
(the center).
All in one carcass.
What is it?

EUROPA ON MAGIC

RIDDLE NO. 102

Releases murky silks
to disorient facts.
Endures the blizzards,
regenerates like lizards.
Weaves the dawn and the dusk
to feed each other cash.
What is it?

- - - - - - - T O W
- - - - - - - T I M

RIDDLE NO. 103

Pure legalese
breaking law to shreds.
Subterranean
above the ground,
dispersing
affordable consolations.
A machine of shadows.
What is it?

_ _ _ _ _ _ Ǝ

RIDDLE NO. 104

Beauty inflates reality.
Twice.
Perpetual flowers looming.
High.
Tears and fears,
sniffing wounds to Future.
Nausea.
Aches and gifts
same time, same space.
What makes this possible?

_ _ _ _ _ _ P
_ _ _ O
O _ _ T

Mihnea Mihalache-Fiastru

is a self-made author dealing with the peculiar and the unknown. He works with image and text, separately and combined.

Mihnea Mihalache-Fiastru trained himself for almost twenty years in docu-fiction writing and journalism. He published stories, essays and articles in foreign and local publications covering a wide range of editorial formats.

He is a content warrior, willing to sacrifice beauty for real wow, favours raw facts to forms and norms, plays silly in writing and not only. In 2015 Mihnea Mihalache-Fiastru created the series Ștrăndooț, a personal journey and exploration of the public pools in Bucharest that was screened in places around the city. In late 2015 and 2016 he created the docu-fiction and urban storytelling web series Șușanele with each episode premiering in expected and unexpected places. In 2016 he co-directed Hot Streets, a full-length experimental film about Bucharest.

Mihnea Mihalache-Fiastru is author of two volumes of documentary prose Tehnologia expunerii universale (2018) and Expres (2019).

He currently works on LIFE`S A BITCH AND THEN YOU DYE VOILÀ!, an intimate photography and text project exploring his personal underworld with some of his lifelong friends: about growing up, living and dying on the streets of their neighborhood and the last days of heroin-consumers old timers.

FRIENDS

Since Iepure ("Rabbit") broke up with Alexandra, Florentina calls me every week or every two weeks. Florentina is Iepure's mom, she worked at The Cotton Factory back in the days. She's a single mom since she and Iepure moved to Pridvorului Street in 1986. They still live together:

> 'Mihnea, he is restless, I can't talk to him anymore, is he doing it again? Is he back on heroin?'

> 'He still takes his treatment, right?', she asks me. 'Does he go to the hospital to take his methadone?'

> 'Yes, he takes his methadone', I tell her.

> 'I found some syringes. I think he will end up in prison again, what do you think?', she asks.

Sometimes I feel uncomfortable, I'm feeding ducks in our park, Tineretului, with my three year old daughter and now I have to say something to Florentina. I don't want to lie to her or anything, but I cannot rat on Iepure, I would never rat on him no matter what, this is us, this is who we are, we've known each other for thirty years. Even Florentina knows I would never rat on him, but what can she do?! What can I do?!

> 'Listen, I think he's not very cautious, I don't know what he does or doesn't do, but there's too many people around your block, comin' in and out of your apartment. Do you understand what I say? I don't think this is good, if you can do something about that, just make him stop bringing them all to your place.'

> 'This is how it was when he went to prison for the second time!', Florentina says.

Iepure went to prison twice, first time for attempted murder and second time for drug trafficking. He was selling methadone to some other trafficker that put him in prison to get his ass out. That guy is dead anyway, he was a long time user, since 1991 or so.

In the summer of 2018 my family and I lived with my parents, for a few months, back in the Tineretului – Văcărești neighbourhood where I grew up. During many of those days I met Iepure and Ilie, Grasu, Papanache, Twig and all the others. At some point I thought of maybe making some pictures of us, those who've been living here since the first days of these blocks, 1986 – 1987. It didn't happen, but in the fall of 2019, jumping the line for the 313 bus—as I was returning to my mom's place from the Big Berceni General Store where I checked some locations for filming—I met Iepure and Alexandra. They were coming back from the Obregia Hospital where they go every day to take their methadone treatment. I don't take methadone, I never did, I quit heroin without substitute. Anyway, we made a couple of pictures. After that, a week later I met Iepure again, this time on my street in another neighbourhood. He was riding a bike, doing some food delivery. We had a moment and we talked about everybody who's alive, about Americanu and Bebe Onosie, Paula's first husband, and about those who passed away. We talked about how sick others are, about HIV and HEP C, the last time I shot and how sure I was that I've got over heroin.

A couple of days later I wrote to Iepure on Facebook with this idea about making a photo series, a sort of long time project about us, our generation of heroin addicts, the first one after the Romanian Revolution of 1989. Iepure was happy and we gathered everyone: Ilie, Paula, Costin, Alexandra, Buze, Andreea, Vierme and some other friends, Sebo, Haljini, Andu, David and some other of their new friends like this guy Pavel who had a big

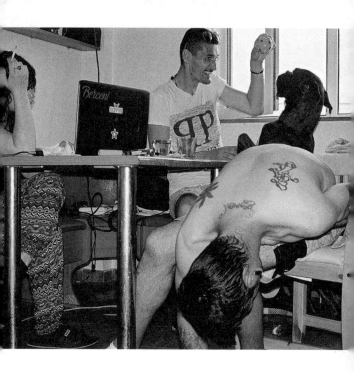

tattoo on his back that became the title of our project or series or book or whatever this will be: 'LIFE'S A BITCH AND THEN YOU DYE VOILA!'

For almost a year we were all out again, talking loudly on public transportation, being stupid, taking silly pictures. We play for the documentary, but we all know this project is just a pose for the joy of being together, always on the run, on the streets of our neighbourhood and in Berceni and Ferentari most of the time.

I did not shoot, I didn't even consider doing it, I see heroin and it doesn't mean anything to me. Orlando died three weeks ago. Life expectancy for heroin users is about 50 years old. So in about 10 years this generation will end. One day Costin, Iepure and I went to Berceni cemetery where my family has its resting place and where Americanu and Bebe, Paula's husbands (and our friends), are buried. Florentina bought a resting place for herself and for Iepure and he wanted to show it to us. We didn't find it, because Iepure was too fucked up to remember where this place was, so we just walked around the cemetery for a while. Costin saw two mobile phones in a car parked with its right window open and he wanted to go at it, but I pulled him over to show him the security cameras:

'What do you think, do they burry them with their jewelry?', Costin asked and we laughed very hard.

'You will go to prison for nothing!', said Iepure.

Three weeks ago small Branea, one of the two Branea brothers that lives in Italy, called Costin worried that he had not heard anything from his brother for two weeks. He thought he might be dead. When I was in the sixth grade and big Branea (Răzvan) was in the seventh grade, I beat the shit out of him out of jealousy. I feel so sorry, I

88

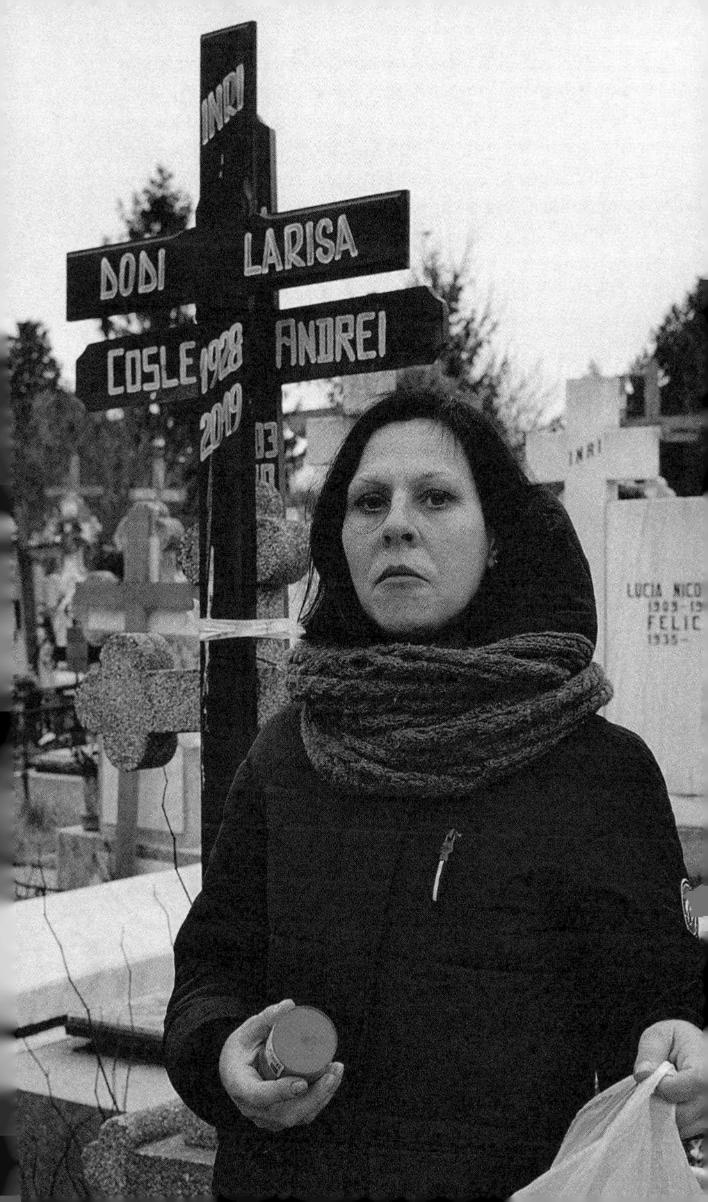
INRI
DODI
LARISA
COŞLE
1928
ANDREI
2019
INRI

never got to tell him that. Anyway, I went out with Costin to look for him in Ferentari and some people told us that they saw him a week or two ago. We thought that maybe he got arrested together with Gina from Ferentari when she went down for trafficking in July. Today I went to my mom to pick up my daughter and I got a call from Costin that we need to go to Branea's funeral, that he was found dead a day ago. The estimated date of death was the 26th of July. That's about when we were looking for him in Ferentari:

'Who died?', my mom asked me, after she heard me on the phone.

'Branea.'

'The small one or the big one?'

Ştefan Constantinescu

(b.1968) is a Romanian filmmaker and artist working with a multiplicity of media. He has directed several short films including *Troleibuzul 92* (2009), presented at the Venice Biennale (IT), *Family Dinner* (2012), selected in Semaine de la Critique in Cannes (FR) and *6 Big Fish* (2013), that premiered in the Pardi di Domani Competition of Locarno IFF (CH).

His feature length documentary *My Beautiful Dacia* (2009), co-authored with Julio Soto, went on to numerous international festivals (IDFA, Jihlava, Montreal, among others) and received the Jury Prize in Documenta Madrid (ES).

Currently he works on postproduction for his feature film *Man and Dog*. He is also working on the artist book *Noah's Ark. An Improbable Space Survival Kit* (co-authored with Corina Ilea).

🌐 http://stefanconstantinescu.com

GORJULUI

In April 2019, Beresheet lunar lander crashed on the Moon.

Several months later, scientists announced that the tardi-grades or "water bears" in the craft's "Lunar Library" could have survived the impact.

The Lunar Library contained a 30 million page archive of human history viewable under microscopes, human DNA and dehydrated tardigrades.

Sabine Bitter & Helmut Weber

Vancouver and Vienna based artists Sabine Bitter and Helmut Weber collaborate on projects addressing the politics of how cities, architecture and urban territories are made into images. Mainly working in the media of photography and spatial installations their research-oriented practice engages with specific moments and logics of the global-urban change as they take shape in neighbourhoods, architecture, and everyday life. Dealing with architecture as a frame for spatial meaning, their ongoing research includes long-term projects such as "Fleeting Territories", "Educational Modernism", "Housing the Social" and "Performing Spaces of Radical Pedagogies" (SSHRC Grant).

In 2004, they formed the urban research collective Urban Subjects with Canadian writer Jeff Derksen. Sabine Bitter is a professor at the School for the Contemporary Arts, Simon Fraser University, Vancouver.

Their work was presented at Museum der Moderne Salzburg (AT), Republic Gallery, Vancouver (CA), Austrian Cultural Forum, New York (US), MAK Center, Los Angeles (US), Museum of Vancouver (CA), freiraum MQ, MuseumsQuartier Vienna (AT), MAXXI - National Museum of Arts, Rome (IT), Contemporary Art Museum, Kumamoto (JP), Tirana International Contemporary Art Biannual (AL), The Power Plant, Toronto (CA), Heidelberger Kunstverein, Heidelberg (DE), NAI, Rotterdam (NL), Museum of Contemporary Art, Belgrade (RS), Kunstraum der Leuphana Universität Lüneburg (DE), MAK, Vienna (AT), NGBK, Berlin (DE), Vancouver Art Gallery (CA), Camera Austria, Graz (AT), Tensta Konsthall (SE).

🌐 http://www.lot.at

HANDLING
HISTORIES

Handling Histories   **Sofia**

Gruia Bădescu

is an urbanist whose research and practice explore the relationship between urban interventions and political transitions, mainly in post-socialist and post-war contexts.

He is an Alexander von Humboldt fellow in Konstanz, Germany, where he is working on a book on architecture and dealing with the past.

Gruia holds a PhD in Architecture from the University of Cambridge, with a dissertation on urban post-war reconstruction in the former Yugoslavia. He has also published on reconstruction in Beirut, on post-socialist urbanism, as well as on urban transformations in the aftermath of dictatorships in Romania, Chile, and Argentina.

He currently lives and works between Konstanz and Bucharest, where he is teaching, developing urban strategies, and working with ATU, an urban think-tank.

I

INTERSECTIONS

When I was eighteen, I was obsessed with foreign guidebooks. *Lonely Planet* and the *Rough Guide* were kings on that list and they both seemed at the time to dismiss Bucharest as a dusty, sprawling city, from which the traveler should run away as soon as possible. Yet the catchphrase of the *Rough Guide* stood with me— Bucharest was Cairo meeting Warsaw and the unlikely child of Paris with Moscow. The latter was, oh yes, stereotypical, a socialist makeover of that Little Paris of the Balkans. But the first juxtaposition was more intriguing. Cairo! Chaos and mystery, noise and, indeed, dust and crumbling facades. Crowds and sociability in packed public spaces. Warsaw? Monolithic socialist blocks of a city that was rebuilt from scratch after a ruthless war. Windswept squares and cold winters. (I later went to Warsaw and found its reconstruction so special actually that I dedicated decades to looking at cities being remodeled after wars). Years of roaming the world and of perpetual returns made me indeed agree: Bucharest is a city of meetings and crossovers, one of intersections.

For each and everyone of us who touched this place, it is a city of very personal intersections with one or more of its parallel universes. There are many worlds coexisting in this city, as in any metropolis. Some might live a lifetime without intersecting the others. Like many complex, divided cities today, it is akin to "the City and the City" of China Miéville, with one world ignoring the others. Yet these worlds are more visible here, in this city of contrasts, than in many segregated places of the West: they stumble in each other's way. As for me, my life is a story of intersections with this city, for which I confess love, and pain. Born here, I was taken to spend my childhood in a Carpathian ballad, then returned to experience first the ugly face of some "anti-newcomer", entitled Bucharest brats in a grey socialist neighbourhood; then as years passed, I discovered some other worlds in it, before leaving for adventures and other magic mountains. I could not imagine being away that much, and, pained by its tormented transformations, I decided to come back and "take a stand" (ah, early youth!), intersecting different worlds that became home. The way that groups morphed, the fluidity and lightness of its sociability, the nets and networks of stories and entanglements, the humour and the beating hearts, all these kept bringing me back. My life has been intertwined, and, while I suffer at times, I cannot let go. It is the city of the eternal comeback.

Bucharest is not a little Paris. Not in its architecture, not in its sociability, not in its contrasts. In Bucharest, the French Beaux-Arts style that arrived with the Paris-loving elites in the 19th century made a remarkable makeover through grand public buildings that amazed traveling

Balkanites. It trickled down to the small houses, replicating the "shells" at the entrances of very unparisian-leafy yards. Yet that is only one aspect of the puzzle. The Francomania triggered the emergence, in response, of the Neo-Romanian style, professing a rootedness in the vernacular architecture of the Subcarpathian Wallachian peasantry and some historic antecedents by Brâncoveanu. Yet it drives comparison to "Eastern expressions", as some of its decorations are to be also found in Anatolian and Persian structures, like *mughrabi* window frames for instance. It bridges Renaissance echoes in Brâncoveanu's style with Byzantium and Iran. Like *sarmale*, claimed as a national dish, yet present from Bosnia to Azerbaijan, this "national architecture" does reflect its locality, yet it is a place of unabashed intersections. Then, next door, you have the *blockhaus* of the 1930s, the geometries of modernity, dreams of the Americas and of new vertical horizons in the previously pancake-wide city. Add to this another modernity, one of the socialist period with its neighbourhoods straight out of Charter of Athens visions, and later it's the 1980s canyon-like avenues of tall buildings hiding the old city behind. This hodgepodge of intersecting influences, visions, and aspirations makes Bucharest worlds apart from Paris. To Haussmanian homogeneity and predictability, Bucharest responds with eclecticism, unparalleled I would say in Europe. Belgrade comes close, yet its historic architecture pales in comparison with the exuberant expression of Bucharest's houses. "Fairytale buildings", one French woman told me, a jungle of faded grandeur and playful intimacy that makes the city look "so old", as a Warsaw artist stuck in the city once confessed.

Yet its eclecticism does not stop at its inherited architecture. It is a place of intersections of ways of being, of urban atmospheres. Martina Löw, a German sociologist, keeps talking about an "intrinsic logic of cities": each city would have a way in which it ticks. Stemming from different histories, spatialities, and clashes of urban visions, cities settle somehow in their own rhythm and disposition. This can be altered, but it somehow endures for a while. From cultures of meeting, of behaving, to how things are done, cities impose somehow, she argues, with their intrinsic logic on urban societies. Others describe this as an "atmosphere", an affective state that shapes moods and modes of being in a city.

Somehow, our brain, as our affective reactions, find echoes of this elsewhere. For me, Belgrade or Beirut feel familiar—while distinctive for so many reasons, there are mirroring atmospheres and affects. With Belgrade, it is perhaps easier to understand. But Beirut also reminds me of Bucharest. To some extent, of course, but this is a pervasive feeling. I try to understand what this familiarity means. It is a sum of historical entanglements—Ottoman and French influences impacted Beirut, and to a more distant, trickled down way, Bucharest. Yet beside the layers of the built environment, it is also the sociability, the social worlds, those bridges of the Balkans and the Middle East that are so enduring, while ignored by many. Bucharest is obsessed with its belonging and longing for Europe. It has been for a while. Yet, it being a place of intersections and different ways of being make it, yes, European, but more, a transnational beast of in-betweenness. Embrace the Balkanness, I say. Maria Todorova, a US historian, once thanked her Bulgarian parents for making her love the Balkans without being proud, nor ashamed of them. It goes the same with the entire Eastern Mediterranean region.

Yet this urban atmosphere has echoes way beyond. A Chilean and a Cuban told me, on separate occasions, that Bucharest feels like a Latin American city in Europe. Grand facades are crumbling, Buenos Aires or Havana style, but more than that, the summer sociability of street life and gathering. Another Chilean, coming from the posh *barrios altos* of the upper middle classes in Santiago, found, however, Bucharest to be way too unsettling to be familiar: the luxury stores next to crumbling facades, the posh ladies next to the beggar, this was too much for the woman used to the manicured lawns of Las Condes, worlds away from Santiago's poor *poblaciones*. Bucharest displays these social and spatial intersections everywhere. It has done for a long time, way before the social mix of the communist-era blocks. On so many older streets, the elongated wagon houses, homes to working class families, lie meters away from the elaborate mansions. It is not just an eclectic hodgepodge of styles, it is also a world of social intersections. Here it departs from the many socially segregated cities of elsewhere, yet for decades now, the middle classes and the rich prefer to withdraw in secluded quarters, to avoid contact and the uncomfortable juxtapositions that defined Bucharest for centuries.

 The summer sociability that my Latin American friends witnessed gives away to the deserted, windswept city of the infamous Bucharest winters, of cold howling winds, dirty snow-dust concoctions of slush and sludge, sidewalks that frustrate every walker, a feel of Siberian gloom and hopelessness. Bucharest's winters make the city despised even by its greatest fans. These are the times of withdrawal and socialisation in smoky indoor spaces. With more than 80% of its population living in housing built in the socialist period, it is now the time that apartment living and central heating come even more to the forefront. These months feature discussions of the presence or absence of hot water, memories of cold flats from the 1980s, and a tendency of overheating, as somehow a late compensation for inherited chilly bones. In Bucharest, the afterlives of socialism and of the initial transition endure.

One of the many labels attached to this city, the one of "post-socialist", also brings together intersecting tropes and images. For decades now there has been a discussion of whether we can still talk about "post-socialist cities". How long is a post- supposed to last? Is this a post-post-socialist city? Will it always be?

For Kiril Stanilov, the post-socialist city in the early 21st century was an intersection of four worlds—the vibrancy and heritage of Western European city centers, the aspirations for car ownership and shopping malls defining North American urban lifestyles, the fast growth (at the time) of East Asian economies, and the dwindling public services and pauperisation of the Global South. Bucharest is a mix and match of this model. The economic boom did not materialise much of an improvement in its appearance. "Heritage" remained an abject word seen as an impediment to real development by many. The even dirtier word was "public", which came under an onslaught of policies and middle class aspirations centered on private worlds. Public education, healthcare, public space, public transport, all suffered a few decades from contempt and disinvestment. The hope of the "commons" found only some scattered fans. Bucharest is not a post-socialist city just because it inherited socialist housing areas and Ceaușescu's idiosyncratic Victory of Socialism Civic Center. It is a post-socialist city because it embodied the drive to

privatise everything, to withdraw the state presence from every life, from every street. The myriads of cables on streets were symptomatic of many disparate agencies and no seeming control—a site indeed to be found in many Latin American urbanscapes. Then, the topic of "commons" came back to the limelight—people, from various social worlds and different political platforms, started asking for it in different ways, from anti-corruption protests to a new left. While antagonistic, they both reclaim a need for more involvement of the public sector, to redefine the social contract. Yet these worlds remain with few intersections and they often vilify each other instead of finding common ground. But, yes, that is a Bucharest thing.

Bucharest has long been a place of intersecting ideas, some coming from abroad, others locally grounded. In the early 18th century, Greek Fanar and Paris met through Bucharest elites, then a long battle between "modernizers" and "tradition-seekers" kept returning. "Forms without the background" said Titu Maiorescu: some were quick to adopt everything that the West provided without critically considering the local context.

Others found the city's Western leanings vile and looked at "local character". In the 1930s, friends at the Criterion Literary Association brought together worldly ideas, from California to India, and wanted Bucharest to graduate from any parochialism and any shadow of 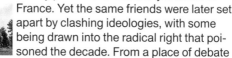 France. Yet the same friends were later set apart by clashing ideologies, with some being drawn into the radical right that poisoned the decade. From a place of debate and exposure to many currents, the city became one of tense ideological struggle. Mihail Sebastian described it well in how intolerance made the city toxic. From a city of intersections, it became one of enmity, where different understandings of purity poisoned its atmosphere. In these polarising contemporary times, let's hope the city keeps its absorbing character without new obsessions about purity of any sorts. That it understands its nature of in-betweenness, of intersections. That its people, through dialogue and more exercises of empathy with the others, aim to understand the complexity of its universes, that are floating, yet forever meet. To repair a broken social contract. A city to be loved, by first of all understanding it.

Ioana Ulmeanu

is a journalist with extensive experience in glossy media. Her current job is as senior editor for ELLE Romania, having already worked for the magazine for a decade.

She passionately believes that she can change the world, if even just a bit, by writing in-depth about topical social issues and contemporary culture, and by giving a platform in her features to progressive voices and ideas.

Forever fascinated by fashion design and the entire phenomena around it, Ioana thinks of fashion as one of the fundamental creative tools to reflect, understand and sometimes critique and predict the shapes of our times.

Ioana Ulmeanu is also recognised for her long-term involvement in human rights activism, with a focus on women's and LGBTQIA+ community rights, tackling issues such as discrimination, equality, access to education, health care and housing.

JOURNEYS

For more than eight years, I intensively used the no. 16 tram to either go to work in Pipera—one of the artificial business districts built chaotically on the outskirts of Bucharest—or to go in the opposite direction, towards the city centre; at least until the current pandemic made us all sit still. We live like trees now, I often say, in admiration but also with some real envy for their mysterious ways.

My apartment is located at the middle of the route, on a busy socialist boulevard marking the way and splitting it into two distinct parts.

I don't remember taking the tram as a child in my hometown, with the notable exception of the journey home after I was hospitalised for a childhood disease. That trip was something of an award, an experience I deserved for patiently waiting for my parents to take me home after two weeks. So I never had an emotional connection to trams, but after I moved to the capital I preferred them to the crowded subway.

The second photo I ever posted on Instagram was taken from tram 16—a view of the lake (Lacul Tei), a magic realm that I must have photographed by then but didn't have an account to post it on.

The third was taken from the tram, too. It was one of a tree that used to grow in a nearby station called Toamnei (Fall). The tree was almost dead by then, but I suppose that the kids in the neighbourhood started hanging dolls in it with a sense of the macabre they weren't

necessarily aware of. Every time I passed by that station, I looked up hoping that I would see another doll had joined the weird nude party. Five dolls had gathered there for what must have been several months, and then they suddenly disappeared. Some time after, the dead tree disappeared, too.

The Toamnei station is located on Strada Viitorului/ The Street of the Future[1], a long and charming slum-like street filled with old small houses where people can be found at all hours of the day. But especially at the beginning of the night, chatting at the gates, crunching on sunflower seeds, perpetually wearing nightgowns and slippers.

It's my favourite street in Bucharest.

With houses seemingly bursting at the seams, deserted gardens and loads of children still playing in the middle of the road, Viitorului makes a colourful scene you would imagine taking place at the periphery. But it is actually still happening day after day quite near the city centre, although its life is starting to fade due to the gentrification taking over the neighbourhood.

To me, this scenery says everything there is to say about Bucharest: its age, its life and inhabitants, its Balkanic origins struggling to survive the specialty coffee shops and the fancy new apartment buildings that are now towering above the rusty roofs. Even the name of the street fits its aesthetics perfectly.

I soon started posting the pictures taken from the tram or while waiting for it at various stations under a

127

1   This is not the accurate translation, but I prefer such an expanded version. "Viitor" means "future" in Romanian, but I insist on including the street part in the translation for the joy of imagining it as the Street of the Future, and not just as a simple street called Future.

hashtag, #tramvaiul16, just to have them filed for easy access. But in doing so I realised my gaze had shifted— I was now looking for subjects, things to post that would translate to the people following me, the allure of the route, the endless row of surprises that fascinated me.

First among them is the lake—also split into two—one part enhancing a civilised, but boring park, now hygienic and empty, but completed with a Ferris wheel, a summer theatre and with its trees topped; the other part is wild, populated by birds, a homeless man (although he does have a home he made by himself out of old ad banners and branches), and fish—as seems to be the case when watching the various fishermen look for prey on summer mornings. Seagulls scream and gather over the lake each season too, forming a noisy crowd, while wild ducks and some coots also cross it, and in some years even swans have found temporary shelter in the area.

Near the lake, the tram is leaving the street, its rails moving on the grass. No obstacles in sight, it gains speed between stations until it arrives back to places where cars are crossing the tracks. In this limited space, the lake and the trees around it make it feel like one is leaving the city, escaping to fabulous destinations where nature has taken over civilisation. I have often found myself wanting to continue the journey: to not get out of the car at my office and just travel without an end station in sight.

Tram 16 and its route are the main reasons why, for many years, I've found the routine of commuting to work truly enjoyable, sometimes even bordering on magical. Living in the middle of a big street with ten storey blocks of flats, I often found myself not noticing seasons chang- ing and time passing. However, from the tram, I could actually see this happening day by day, witnessing, near the lake, dramatic changes of scenery and feelings. But one day there was an incident that broke the spell for me: a fox was killed in a collision with the tram. The poor thing must have been disturbed by the changes in her habitat, with big constructions popping up nearby the wilder area of the lake. That was a sad experience to carry with me on 16, and for a long time I didn't enjoy the trips as before, seeing how in the race for profits and spaces to build close to "nature" the city engulfs the fragile remains of wilderness.

The trams on line 16 are old and something is always broken inside them. In the summer the temperature can reach more degrees than humans can comfortably bear and in winter there may be some heat, if you're lucky. But then there's always the humid and comforting haze coming from the breath of the passengers, many of them children or teens from the schools on the route. At the hour I'm going to work, many of the passengers are poor Roma women living near the lake and already heading back home, from the market, their bags filled with more bread than I can imagine entire hungry crowds devouring. With time, we started saying hi or smiling when we saw each other. Every now and then things get heated—white passengers shouting profanities and threatening to shoot them, just because they are Roma. When did a group of women carrying bags and speaking loudly turn into a menace?

I never went to see their neighbourhood.

In fact, it took me years to stop along the way and to explore the lake and its surroundings because for a very long time I just stared out the window or simply inside the tram, at people.

People are fascinating. First there are the guest stars, appearing there never to be seen again, like the girl with blue hair that I only saw once, or various old men going nowhere. Then there are the regulars: the old lady selling nail-clippers and sponges from a raffia bag and the young man with poor eyesight, carrying a large wooden bat and mumbling, terrifying passengers, albeit inoffensively. Then there are the Roma youngsters who always seem to be up to something, but are just cheerful and mischievous. There are the elders, endlessly talking politics and fishing and always disagreeing on both issues. And, of course, there are some like me, going to work, with their headphones on or talking mostly about boring work related issues. For some reason, I always felt I shouldn't photograph the faces of the people in the tram. Sometimes one of these regulars just disappears, never to be seen again taking the tram. I like to imagine they just moved to another neighbourhood. But in this tram such a disappearance can also mean people going to jail, children being taken away by Child Protection services, and, of course, death.

Death is often talked about, especially when it comes to the people who, for a long while, have been traveling from the outskirts towards a hospital near my house that hosts the only state funded methadone clinic in the city. They are addicts and the treatment is always scarce— being so, it often becomes a commodity and the centre of long and violent debates. The addicts are often young, their eyes depleted and talking about dead friends. Death, in their discussions, isn't some dramatic exit leaving others in tears. It's just a fact of life, as common as putting on clothes to go out in the morning. At some point they disappeared, too. But when I walk the streets along the route and I see syringes on the sidewalk, I take it as a good sign. They are still here, somewhere, cramped in houses with plywood at the windows.

Birth is also a subject as someone is always giving birth or going to some hospital to visit a relative or friend who did so, and the event must be discussed and celebrated loudly. Then there are the women breastfeed-ing and carrying their babies in strollers, struggling to get them on the tram.

To confirm the discussions, there are always children on the tram, of various ages. Most of them are very young and aren't accompanied by adults. They are happy and free and dirty and mostly running around laughing and using the hand-grabs to sway and swing; the elders look away disapprovingly.

The kids are usually travelling towards the lake, and on summer mornings I sometimes see them plunging in the water. In winters, I can see them skating on improvised contraptions.

The second part of the route, starting from my station (one that even has a song dedicated to it) and going to the city centre, is equally contrasting and, to me, very sentimental.

There's the odd vintage luxury car appearing every now and then in a poor area, lacking registration plates; the new apartment buildings announcing exceptional, sustainable design, sitting next to derelict homes. There's poverty and then there are the young professionals bringing their cars, strollers, children and complaints into the neighbourhood.

At some point along the way, the tram takes a turn crossing a wide old boulevard, Dacia, that leads to the centre, with embassies and huge manor-like buildings guarding the large street.

I realised some years ago that the sharp turn of the road must mark the exact spot where a fictional event took place, the accident that put into motion the action from my favourite teenage novel, first published in 1940. One day, looking out the window (it must have snowed, but I cannot really recall that, it may also be a fake memory triggered by the scene in the book), I remembered the almost exact words describing the location in the first pages: "I always get off when the tram's moving. Otherwise it does not work. I live near here, on Bulevardul Dacia, and the number 16 tram only stops on Donici or on Vasile Lascăr. It's too far away. That's why I get off at the turn, where the tram goes onto Orientului. Not just me. Everybody who lives around here does it. And nothing ever happens. Except for today… I don't know how it happened." (excerpt from Mihail Sebastian's *The Accident*, 2011, Biblioasis, translated from Romanian by Stephen Heninghan). There's a station now in that place, so no accident could happen again.

I started looking for a building resembling the main character's home, as if the accident and the story that unfolds after it were real, unable to discern between fact and fiction, just as the characters from the book did at some point. But knowing the writer must have taken the exact same route decades ago and hoping that, as time has a different meaning along this way, I could at some point find myself lost in a temporal bubble taking me back to those times.

It's not as if they were good times—Sebastian was Jewish and wrote extensively in his diary about the fascism taking over Romania in the war times, the riots and pogroms, the injustice and hate that he faced every day from his far-right colleagues and friends in intellectual circles. He was as tormented and complicated as his characters, things that drew me towards his books in high school. But there's also love in his stories. And then there's hope.

I discovered the connection to the novel by chance, but it brought another layer to the feelings I developed for the tram and its stories, the route seemingly leading me through entire worlds, and taking me to places that exist in imagination alone.

There are real places, too… Two of my closest friends moved along the route and I used the tram even more coming and going. Sometimes I missed the last one during the night and had to walk home through this space that could seem dangerous, but to me is just a familiar and much loved territory.

There's beauty along the way, but it doesn't come from the buildings or the trees, but from the countless clashes between worlds; the constant movement of the people, their worn faces in the evening or on hot summer days, their words and their actions, their continuous flow.

When the rails were repaired, the end of the line in the centre changed several times in the years I've been a regular. But it always remained in the same area, on the edges of a loop, near an old church or in a vacant square used as a market or a parking lot, where an old queer painter put together a gorgeous open air art gallery, hanging his works on the bordering walls or simply drawing on them, or on the ground, the trash bins, everywhere.

His name is Murivale, I later found out, and he also had some exhibitions in the more traditional white cubes. Though I've never seen one of those, I was endlessly fascinated by the ones he displayed in that station, works scribbled with chalk on the ground, in puddles of rain or dog (could be human) pee. I spent a lot of time watching them, the auras of saints sitting next to the faces of queer celebrities and local gay rights activists, some of them friends of mine gathering right around the corner, at the headquarters of their organisation, in a building that used to house a police station and its creepy dungeons back in the day.

Out there, in that temporary station, the painter displayed so much beauty for everyone to see that his generosity deeply moves me every time. As some of his paintings fade with the seasons, the flowers he planted occupy the scarce soil near the pavement and start spreading. They're seeds of a future jungle that I imagine taking over the city when all civilisation is gone, but the tram 16 still continues its uninterrupted glide on the rails.

Decebal Scriba

is an artist approaching many different media such as drawing, photography, installation, performance and video art, with sustained activity in the sphere of conceptual art. He is living and working in France since 1991.

"The coordinates of his works open up many levels, including, on the one hand, that of the analysis of the systems of representation and production and reproduction of space, alongside that of the conceptualization of the (visual, mathematical and textual) signification systems and, on the other hand, at the level of a private, interiorized and nearly existential assumption of the artistic act." (Cristian Nae, *A Field of Possibilities – Decebal Scriba and The Semiotics of Appearance*)

Starting with 1974 his work was presented in landmark exhibitions in Romania: *Situation and Concept* (1974), Atelier 35, Bucharest; *Writing* (1980), *Space-Object* (1982), *Space-Mirror* (1986), Institute of Architecture, Bucharest; *Experiment in Romanian Art after 1960*, The National Theater, Bucharest (1996), but also in projects abroad.

Alongside Nadina Scriba and a group of friends, he initiated *House pARTy*, editions I (1987) and II (1988), an alternative event in Bucharest that later turned into a legendary video document of that era.

In recent years, his work was presented at CC Strombeek (BE), Salonul de Proiecte, Bucharest (RO), Paris Photo International (FR), BF15 Gallery, Lyon (FR), Kunsthalle, Mulhouse, (FR), Art Encounters Biennial, Timișoara (RO), tranzit.ro/Bucharest (RO), Propaganda Gallery, Warsaw (PL), Plan B Gallery, Berlin (DE), Anne-Sarah Bénichou Gallery, Paris (FR), Anca Poterașu Gallery, Bucharest (RO), Calina Gallery, Timișoara (RO).

KINSHIP

BUCHAREST URBAN DESIGN REPORT 1972

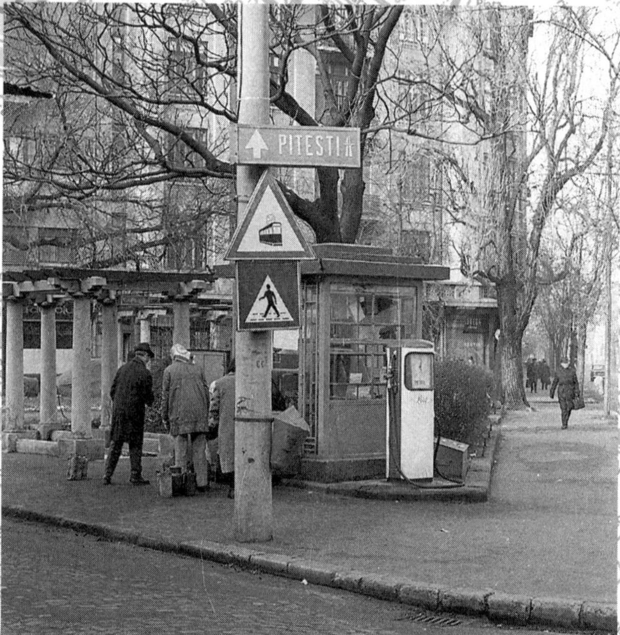

- Incoherent design for kiosks and news stands
- Obsolete public payphones
- Street delivery of hazardous substances

- Cluster of uncomfortable public benches
- Taxi station and cluster of public payphones

- Chaotic mix of kiosks & phone booths
- Unattractive display systems for outdoor announcements

● Waiting/ Public transport shelter without schedule

- Obsolete tram
- Misplaced road mirror
- Erratic/ Eclectic taximeter network
- Gas station running out of fuel

- Misplaced or redundant signalectic
- Improvised signs for construction sites
- Public transport information almost impossible to update

Sillyconductor

is one of the monikers of Cătălin Matei, a Romanian sound artist living and working in Bucharest.

Sillyconductor's main focus has always been on classical music and its relationship with mathematics: projects such as *Ventichitara* (a self-made improvisation instrument built out of USB fans), *100 Catronomes* (a golden rendition of Ligeti's *Poeme Symphonique* employing 100 Maneki Neko cats) or the *Pianosaurus* (a post-modern mechanical piano) explore overlapping shapes between technology, classical music and humour. The *Ondiocytherium*, a double body sound object is an instrument that self-destructs over time, inspired by the Laser Doppler Vibrometry and different techniques for speeding up the aging process of materials. Recently he's been working with artificial instinct as generative source, writing music for theatre or games, creating sound installations and workshops for hearing impaired kids or employing novel recording techniques for church organs in Transylvania as part of the *MetaOrganum* project.

He performed or his works were presented at V&A Museum, London (UK), MAK Museum, Vienna (AT), Konzerthaus Berlin (DE), Ars Electronica, Linz (AT), MNAC Bucharest (RO). Sillyconductor played festivals such as Unsound Festival, Krakow (PL), TodaysArt Festival, The Hague (NL), Transmediale, Berlin (DE), Arma17, Moscow (RU), Insomnia Festival, Tromso (NO), Eurobeats Festival, Washington (US), Le Placard Festival, Antwerp (BE), Rokolectiv Festival, Bucharest (RO), Periferias Festival, Huesca (ES), Crack Festival, Rome (IT), Simultan Festival, Timișoara (RO).

🌐 https://soundcloud.com/sillyconductor

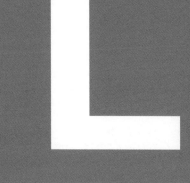

LAWNMOWER
DYSPHORIA

To my surprise, 2020 was the year that had me travel a lot, notably in the more pastoral areas of Romania. From Letea to Negrești-Vaslui, from Sovata-Mureș to Cîrțisoara-Sibiu, Slănic-Moldova to Tulcea, recording forest sounds from Iași or Brașov, just about forgetting the smell of car fumes.

If there was one thing that crept progressively into my conscience until it became intolerable, like a crowned virus, it was the one ominous sound in all these land-scapes: the portable lawnmower, my soon-to-be source of depression, anxiety and agitation.

It was amusing at first, but then, as with any sound that grasps your attention and never lets go, it became tiring. After its fifth appearance, I became more and more annoyed by its continuous presence, and it began to feel like a poorly planned prank.

Living in Bucharest for more than twenty years now, I've become accustomed to all sorts of fierce sounds. Sirens, helicopters, all sorts of military planes passing over the city for fly-pasts, fireworks, construction works, accidents, screams, car horns, protests, etc. But I always thought that these were provocative noises, stuff that I could record for later use, vessels for rich harmonic content and short stories of marvelous evolution. I still find myself instinctively reaching for the recorder when I hear a bomber plane approaching from the distance and I am particularly pleased with a recording of a taxi driver's protest when nearly 100 cars were honking at the same time, creating a fabulous drone that would shape-shift every second. On top of that, not a single year has passed without recording the New Year's Eve fireworks. In the end it's just diversity and surprise.

The sound of the lawnmower, on the other hand, is something else. It deeply irritates me. There's no scare, no surprise. Its monotonous sound triggers me on a deep, visceral level. It's an instant provocation by a giant mosquito that startlingly and repeatedly ruins my sleep. Or my lunch. Or my stroll. You see where I'm going with this.

Thirty, twenty or even ten years ago, the countryside was a synonym for quiet. It was a mirage of silent nights with one single dog barking conveniently in the distance, birds chirping discretely during the day, perhaps a cowbell or two seasoning the ambience with Zen-like overtones. One would get out of the car upon arrival from the city and marvel at the peace and quiet surrounding these uncomfortable but remote cottages. The only mechanical sounds that would hover as a reminder of the present day would be the chainsaw. I didn't expect people to use axes so it didn't bother me that much, except for when I was trying to record alphorns.

But things have changed. It's like we're part of an industrial revolution that has taken villages by storm altogether. And it's the small industrial revolution of cheap lawnmowers and small electric tools. Affordability has empowered any villager with at least five electric or petrol-chomping tools. Grass wars were never so loud. The everlasting conflict with vegetation now has its own soundtrack. And I bloody hate it. I'm with dandelions on this one.

There should be a scientific explanation for my uncontrollable disgust. It's definitely not a posh assumption that rural inhabitants are still using their Iron Age apparatus. And it's definitely not an "Oh my god, I'm a sound artist, I live in an anechoic chamber and I carefully curate my sound environment with the help of angels" sort of theory. I've been successfully coping with one of the noisiest capitals in the world. Why, oh why, out of all the sounds, do I find the lawnmower the most disturbing? Is it because of expectations? Is it because the promised silence of the green meadows is constantly compromised by this sound of tiny motocross events with a single contestant? Is it because they are small motors and their puny but penetrating output offers such little variation? Is it because there is proper silence surrounding the lawn-mower and that in itself amplifies the noise to demigod proportions? Or is it simply an issue of aesthetics?

Many years back I read an interview with Delia Derbyshire, who was part of the BBC's Radiophonic Workshop team of sound pioneers. In that interview there was one thing that stuck in my head. When the first synthesizers appeared and were brought to their studio, they had very little appeal. Synth sounds, albeit unheard of, only reminded them of a cat chewing a bee. The basic waveforms, the sine wave, the square wave, the triangle or the sawtooth, were nothing more than different types of insects, having limited flexibility. Delia Derbyshire was accustomed to using organic material, real samples, voices or foley sounds that were recorded onto tape and manipulated through tedious methods: cut up and sped up, slowed down or multiplied through different tech-niques. But it was analogue so the result was never a bee. And it sounded as organic as the original source, perhaps even more.

Doing a bit of research about my noisy nemesis, I came across a series of graphics included in either user manuals or mowing catalogues and things started to make sense. And then it dawned on me. Looking at the available accessories it quickly became clear what the problem was. The included knives resembled all the basic types of oscillators available on a monosynth since the beginning of time. (fig.1) Sawtooth in the 8 teeth one? Square in the 4 teeth one? Sine wave as the round thing? All there. (fig.2) And then there was the 1.7 horsepower farty motor. I pulled out an audio editor for a visual representation. Marvel at the majestic complexity of a Bell Helicopter (fig.3), which would usually have me on my knees decibel-wise compared to a Ruris Dac 210 mower (fig.4).

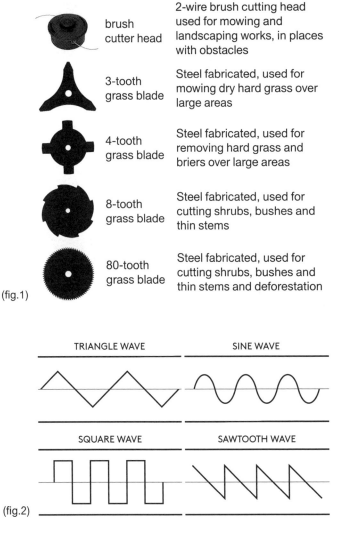

brush cutter head	2-wire brush cutting head used for mowing and landscaping works, in places with obstacles
3-tooth grass blade	Steel fabricated, used for mowing dry hard grass over large areas
4-tooth grass blade	Steel fabricated, used for removing hard grass and briers over large areas
8-tooth grass blade	Steel fabricated, used for cutting shrubs, bushes and thin stems
80-tooth grass blade	Steel fabricated, used for cutting shrubs, bushes and thin stems and deforestation

(fig.1)

TRIANGLE WAVE

SINE WAVE

SQUARE WAVE

SAWTOOTH WAVE

(fig.2)

(fig.3)

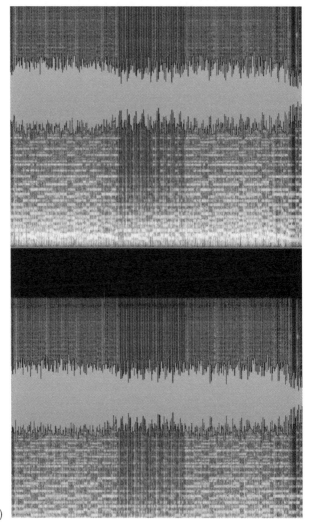

(fig.4)

The mower is petty, boring, grainy and offers absolutely zero challenges for your acute senses. It's like fast Morse code. It's just there, mindlessly popping away with its two stroke engine. I know it's not a fair comparison but sounds are competing for your attention in the wild, just as screaming coherently offers an advantage over mumbling unintelligibly. And then there's the low frequency oscillator, adding a bit of variation to synth sounds in a wah-wah manner, perfectly replicated by the swinging left-right-left movement of the mowing expert, trying to overpower every bit of green on the blue planet.

What is the most popular and loudest sound in Bucharest? The sirens. Do they bother me? No, because thanks to the Doppler effect and to the actual role of emergency vehicles, a siren is built to be just coming and going, never beeping idiotically in one place. Its oscillating tones were carefully chosen for this, you know. Unless it had at least two tones, you would mistake it for a regular car horn. It's usually just a one minute sound ride, unless you're a patient.

And the mower is just the start. In my travels I have seen people using electrical air compressors to inflate the wheels of their horse carriages and then horse away. I have seen them using electrical grinders to sharpen their scythes and then scythe away, in complete silence. Rural Romania is going through the second stage of mechanisation. Cheap, as it is, an industrial revolution powered by discount offers and seductive red plastics, hypermarkets contributing with affordable methods of turning people into half-robots. I may be paranoid. It's cheap empowerment, but I feel like this everlasting fight with vegetation isn't always about survival, but decor. People sure do like their machines and they use them for anything.

One the other hand, the rustling of the poplar leaves is one of the most eloquent representations of white noise. It brings wind to completion. Please find a poplar and listen to it. Are we in a white noise versus sawtooth rural dilemma? Whereas in the electronic world, both types of sound can be combined for a more intriguing result, in the agrarian world, white noise finds itself in an inequitable disadvantage. And the tree is utterly defenseless.

This brings us to the eternal question: if a poplar falls near a village and there is no one to hear it, will it make a sound? The answer is yes; the sound will be subsequent and made out of several hours of incessant sawtooth bursts.

I miss my sirens.

Prosper Center

is a Romanian brand that nurtures an ongoing exchange of influences between fashion and the wider society, in a considerate and sustainable way. The pieces of clothing are locally produced and inspired by their surroundings, mixing global street fashion with complex Eastern European aesthetics, reflecting contradictory and diverse information flows like ourselves. Prosper Center deconstructs and reassembles parts of garments and patterns into a mix of performative streetwear.

The pieces recombine elements of recreational wear while also adding a theatrical, stage-like feature that reflects the increasingly fictional nature of our reality. The designs often use cross-stitch embroideries inspired by computer games, popular culture, politics, artworks and stock market graphics which are embedded as decorative commentary on a non-chronological time, where past, present and future come together into one hybrid image.

In 2016 Prosper Center collaborated on a fashion collection with Tranzit Iași art space which was presented at Sala Polivalentă in Iași, and in 2017 it presented its Spring Summer 2018 collection during Mercedes Benz Fashion Days Kyiv. In the same year the designer behind the brand, Andrei Dinu, was nominated for the Best Young Designer by ELLE Magazine. Andrei Dinu studied costume and set design.

He often collaborates with artist Alexandra Pirici on various works which were presented at Art Basel Messeplatz (CH), Berlin Biennale (DE), New Museum NY (US) among others. In 2011 he was the designer of the Romanian pavilion at the Prague Quadriennal of Performance Design and Space (CZ).

🌐 https://prosper-center.squarespace.com

MEMORY

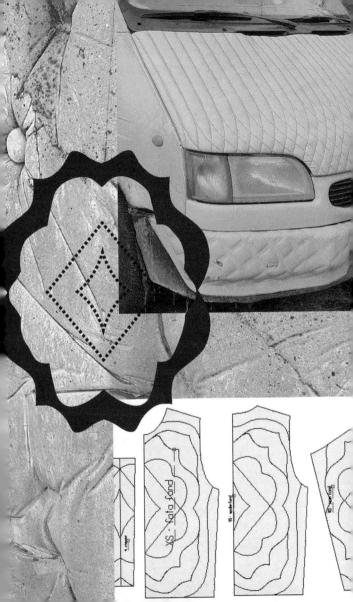

"I'm Telling You Stories. Trust Me"[1]

Interview with Ioana Nemeș

by Stuart Aarsman

Originally published in Idea magazine no 20 (2005) p. 39-51.

[1]   Jeanette Winterson, in *Art Objects – Essays on Ecstasy and Effrontery*, London, Johnathan Cape Random House, 1995, p. 71.

Ioana Nemeș

(Bucharest, 1979 – New York, 2011) is one of the most acknowledged and exhibited Romanian artists of her generation.

Her artistic research was fueled by the necessity to visualize and communicate as clearly as possible the hidden mechanism behind linguistic, visual, and psychological systems that define us.

Ioana participated in the Istanbul Biennial (TR), U-Turn Copenhagen (DK), Prague Biennial (CZ) and Bucharest Biennale 2 (RO).

Nemeș's work has been exhibited internationally in museums and contemporary art centers such as Art in General, NY (USA), Secession, Vienna (AT), Smart Project Space, Amsterdam (NL), Kunsthalle Fridericianum, Kassel (DE), Royal College of Art, London (UK), Brukenthal Museum, Sibiu (RO), Salonul de Proiecte, Bucharest (RO), Eastside Projects, Birmingham (UK), Caixaforum Barcelona (ES), ArtEncounters, Timișoara (RO), MNAC Bucharest (RO), The Museum of Sculpture at Krolikarnia Warsaw (PL), Uj Gallery, Budapest Museum (HU), KIM?, Riga (LV), BOZAR, Brussels (BE), Bunkier Sztuki, Kraków (PL) as well as in publications like *100 New Artists* (publisher Laurence King) and *Romanian Cultural Resolution* (publisher Hatje Cantz). She was a resident at Art in General, NY (2011), IASPIS, Stockholm (2010), The Romanian Cultural Institute, London (2007) and Kulturkontakt, Vienna (2004).

Ioana Nemeș was also member of several collectives working in art, fashion and interior design contexts: Kilobase Bucharest (2011), Apparatus 22 (2011), Rozalb de Mura (2005-2010) and Liste Noire (2004-2011).

⊕ http://ioananemes.ro

STUART AARSMAN is a writer and independent curator. He studied art and philosophy at Rietveld Academy, Amsterdam. MA at Central Saint Martin College of Art and Design, London. Writing for Metropolis M, Baby, RE-, Blvd, Afterall, Frieze etc. *All the Facets of the Same B.* – philosophical essay about art & consumerism published in 2002 by Artimo/Gijs Stork.

I met Ioana in a restaurant in Amsterdam. It was just after her opening in Ellen's gallery. We all ordered pizza; it was one of these Turkish or Arabic restaurants. Some of us started to ask Ioana some questions. I was amazed by the seriousness and keenness of her answers to our questions and decided I have to talk about her works. We exchanged email addresses. I wanted to take advantage of my going through Bucharest on my way to Istanbul to meet Ioana again. More exactly, I wanted to interview her. We decided together, in fact Ioana did, that there would be three locations for the interview, not only one: a sports hall, a dam and a movie hall; three different spaces but which meant for her something more than simple public spaces to go on weekends. We established together the topics we wanted to explore in the interview and attached to each location a specific issue: colours & cubes for the sports hall, Romanian context for the dam, and fiction & reality for the movie hall.

LOCATION: FLOREASCA SPORTS HALL
SUBJECT: COLOURS & CUBES

Floreasca sports hall is located in a nice Bucharest neighbourhood. In order to get there, you have to cross a quiet stretch of alleys and green spots winding among old villas with no more than three storeys. The atmosphere is so serene, you wouldn't say you are so close to the 15 story colossus of the Romanian Television—the hottest spot that Romanians tried to conquer during the revolution of '89. The sports hall is also rather old; the field is not even in compliance with the regulations because the space between the stands and the field is much too narrow and there are frequent accidents. The dome is fabulous; built in old fashioned style, of wooden arcades combined with glass that impregnate this space with a certain bourgeois spirit. Ioana arrived at 12 o'clock sharp, she asked me if she was late and confessed she hated to be late. She looks quite sleepy, maybe because of her slovenly clothes: a blouse made of shiny bluish brown velvet, slippery on her body, beautifully tailored, plush velvet brown trousers, very puffed from the waist and tight on the leg under the knee, and some deep purple flip-flops.

Stuart Aarsman:
How come you didn't enter the main door?

Ioana Nemeş:
I used to pass through this corridor when I came to trainings. This was only for players, referees and coaches. It's a very narrow corridor and it reminds me of the passage ways that lead out to the sand circle of a Spanish bullfighting arena. The same tension that accumulates along the corridor to break out in the hall.

SA:
It's very beautiful.

IN:
I like it when it's quiet, like now, when there is nobody.
You know what I'm thinking of? Of that sound made
by the ball when it is hit to the freshly clean floor, of the
sound we hear in the *In the Musicals* tune sang by Björk
or Selma in *Dancer in the Dark*. It's interesting to see how
a sports hall has its own pulsations when it is full, the
public is in rapture and the atmosphere is on fire, or when
it is deserted, in a way emptied of its functionality.

SA:
Or when it is half full, when there are only trainings
going on, with no public.

IN:
Then it is something very intimate, because it's only
yours, you don't share it with anybody, you can hear
all the noises you make, how your sneakers squeak on
the floor, the noise made by the ball if you put too much
clister on it.

SA:
What's clister?

IN:
It's a sort of natural glue, made of pine resin, transparent,
with a very penetrating odour. You put it on the ball for
a better adherence. It is used, as far as I know, only in
handball.

SA:
Let's talk about colours.

IN:
And about cubes.

SA:
Yes, and about your project, *Monthly Evaluations*, that you presented in Amsterdam. But I would like to place the topic in a wider context. You were once saying something about the changes in perspective brought by your conversion from photography to sculpture and literature. Even though you didn't want to show me any of your photos, I searched on the internet and I found some. Why this aversion to photography?

IN:
My aversion is not indiscriminate, all-inclusive. I don't have anything against photography as artistic language, it's just that I've become more skeptical towards this language, its diplomatic nature gets on my nerves, the fact that it doesn't allow you to be very direct, with the exception of the documentary genre, but that can be staged too.

SA:
Where does this skepticism come from?

IN:

Part of it comes from the theory and philosophy books about photography I've read after I finished school—well I didn't quite finished it yet, because I still have to defend my thesis, but after I didn't go to school so frequently. My naïve optimism from my first years in school, that I could hold a rather good duplicate of things, situations and spaces around me, that I can "steal" it and keep it only for me vanished when I was introduced to the realistic part of photography, with its history, its genres and techniques. I couldn't ignore its consistency, nor could I pretend to only visit it. I found myself in its house and had to behave accordingly. Therefore I became more conscious, I started to stage the situations that appeared in my photos. Then I tried to push the limits of seriality when I photographed (throughout the course of one whole year) the window of a fashion boutique in Bucharest's historical centre. For one year I turned myself with pleasure into a psychopath stalker, who registered night after night the changes in the shop window.

SA:

Is this *Behind the Window Shopper* project?

IN:

Yes, and it is the book I have to make as my thesis. Then came the residency at KulturKontakt in Vienna, where I did nothing else but read as much as I could. The people there expected me to take some photos, which kind of irritated me, so I've decided to exhibit some A4 sheets in which I meticulously exposed how I had spent the money from the scholarship, a sort of financial statement on every day in which I enumerated all the items bought during my residence. It was in Vienna that I've exhibited for the first time something other than photography, and I must admit I felt relieved.

SA:
What kind of photography did you used to make?

IN:
All kinds of stuff. From my "naïve" period, details of common everyday objects which, through distorted perspective and context, changed their identity in a way. I was paying much attention to the composition, materiality and colours. My pictures from back then are very colourful, small, and with a minimum dose of slightly sarcastic humour. Soon after I've received various encouragements and congratulations, I realised something was wrong. That everything was too facile. That this funny approach was not leading anywhere. Then I started making pictures that looked in some way like fashion photographs, but I soon abandoned this genre too. I thought they were too superficial, with a too big risk of being perceived as more than they really were. And finally, I came to doing what I said I would never do: landscapes. Nature, trees, sun, water, mist, a lot of mist, rain. All the meteorological register.

SA:
Why did you say you'll never do landscapes?

IN:
Because I don't like recipes, in general. Because I realize I react quite strongly to what is happening around me, I have a quick feedback and it would have been too easy only to push the button. All too much gratuitous. Nature by excellence offers itself gratuitously to us. It's present everywhere, you only have to notice it. It's incredibly positive.

[In a rather small room, on the left wall there are some images glued with paper scotch. Most of them are clippings from magazines, postcards or cheap photo-copies made after colour photos. Cold, artificial, neon light. Even if glued spontaneously, in time, the images are carefully arranged in three rows. Each row is made of 7 or 8 images, and there are a total of roughly 25 images. In the first row, the following images are stringed: a cream sculpture by Gabriel Orozco on a pale grey background, a sheet with colour index prints on the back of which is written, "I'll never take any picture unless I fully understand what I'm doing and why", an iPod with one pink side and another one golden, a black and white portrait of Virginia Woolf from 1935, taken by Man Ray, a drawing with three rocks, pink, black and grey, clipped from Metropolis M magazine, a British pattern with roses for Marimekko bed linen, and a piece of brownish paper on which is scribbled in pencil, "all this solid rapture".]

SA:
Will you show me your landscape photos?

IN:
They are in a very beautiful series—that frightens me a little—called "Twin Pictures", which I only exhibited in a shortened version in Hungary. They are double land-scapes, made in parallel by two persons. "Landscape" is a too generous word, for even some blocks can create

the feeling of a natural landscape. Architecture is an artificial nature. I have a lot of photos, tens of negatives I haven't exhibited for many reasons. Maybe some day I will dig them out and restore them morally.

SA:
How did your interest move, from photography to sculpture and literature?

IN:
During the four years in faculty I only studied photography and I'm not sure whether this monopoly was useful or not. I would have liked to experiment with scenography, fashion, theatre, sculpture, journalism, make-up, cinematography, music, marketing, design, and so on.

SA:
You are talking about more than a multidisciplinary school. I don't know if there are such schools.

IN:
I would have liked such a school, even if it had to last for eight years. A school with such a mobility, where one could study exactly the fields one wanted. Educational systems lack such flexibility.

SA:
Now you can really study anything you want on the internet, there are a lot of online courses. It's true you can't compare them to a regular school, but nevertheless there is a tendency towards flexibility. Why did you choose sculpture and literature?

IN:

For their direct language. Object vs. image, or word vs. image. I'm in search of something that wouldn't leave too much space for interpretations. Information must get from one end to the other without too many perturbations. The transmitter and the receiver, even if they can switch their places, must count on the clarity and precision of the message. I try to avoid viruses as much as possible.

SA:
Such as?

IN:

Such as the means of manipulating the image. Such as the technical luggage every field is equipped with, that set of rules that you should follow if you want to create a good product. Such as composition rules, material use regulations, assembling rules, the aesthetic rules of a movie screenplay, rules related to exposing a good product, promotion and communication rules, and those related strictly to language, to the terms we use. There are a lot of poles established by the majority for the sake of the majority, for whom a good product equals a less delicious apple, but which fits perfectly within standards, size, colour and weight. The word "must" fascinates me. Many times it is used out of inertia: one must respect one's parents, one must belong to a well known religion, one must forgive, one must begin one's sexual life no later than 18, one must not skip breakfast, one must use a hydrating cream, preferably L'Oréal with SPF and Q10, because it seems that nothing is hazardous. You must read certain books, see certain movies, you must have children. You must get married, have your own house and a job. By the way, why must one have a job?

SA:
You mustn't do all the things you counted.

IN:
Why mustn't you?

SA:
Because you can choose, you have this option, to choose what you want to do.

IN:
I've read somewhere that it is good to have a job mainly because you have to give something back to the society in which you were born, and secondly, in order to have money to live, to buy a house, clothes, food. From this point of view, society seems to me very cruel, like a possessive and jealous mother, and this endless exchange, quantitatively speaking, between consumerism and production seems very tiresome. Why should I be indebted to the society in which I was born?

SA:
Because you are using its infrastructure, its laws, its subway and its buildings, aren't you?

IN:
Yes, but you pay for it, don't you? You pay the rent and the monthly subway pass. You pay taxes. It's a very passionate relationship, in which both partners use each other as much as they can. That's why trespassing the rules of society seems to me the most exciting thing possible. You betray its trust in you and you destroy its expectations. What can be more romantic than that?

SA:
Now that's a very interesting relationship, between you and this society!

IN:
Yes, I'm still searching, trying to understand my role as an artist, as a producer of cultural objects, producer of new perspectives and points of view. And I really don't understand, why must I produce something? Why can't I just consume? Anyway this is the thing I like to do best. Why, after having consumed books, movies, magazines, artworks, interior design, opinions and commentaries, do I have to say my opinion on what I've just consumed? And, since I'm an artist, should it be expressed in another work of art?

SA:
Well, because there is a balance also found in nature and in Buddhism, the middle way or the golden path, teaching you that whatever is consumed must be replaced. Anyway this balance is rather precarious and if there is too much swinging a lot of natural calamities will appear. It's a basic principle, isn't it? And since everything functions according to this principle for so many years, that means that it is worth something. Let's talk about literature, I've seen on the blue wall the "accidental meeting" between you and Virginia Woolf. Why V. Woolf?

IN:
In the Amsterdam exhibition I've only exhibited the month of October. Out of pure coincidence I've fallen upon the books of Virginia Woolf in a local shattered library, and I decided that I must—you see, this word again, read all her novels, essays, journals . You have to know that the books from our district libraries date back to the

Ceaușescu era, rarely something new is brought, so that day I left for the library with no enthusiasm at all. I was looking for some modern writers. Virginia Woolf appears on the blue wall because I've read a lot about and by her that month. And she is one of my favourites writers.

SA:
Why?

IN:
Because she is incredibly strong, intellectually sharp, even cutting for those post Victorian times. Even though her writings are velvety, translucent and civilised, which is specific to the materiality of that era, you can find, in the underground, a black, critical and mischievous river, that stream of consciousness, that awakening and cold look on psychological life, on time and the changes it causes. I've also read her journals, unfortunately the older version censored by her husband, Leonard, and I was fascinated by the almost masochistic seriousness with which she used to analyse her writing and her technical development of language, by the importance she gave to the word, not to its meaning, but to its music. She writes very musically, you know, following a rhythm, not a plot. She is interested in the word itself, in what it contains more than its baptising effect, that of naming things, people or emotions. I think she loves this very solid substance of a word, emptied of any link to anything recognisable. I love her sexual and material independence, and the essay "A Room of One's Own" is simply fabulous for those conservative times. Then I think her endeavours to register, dissect, understand and depict impalpable things such as life or time are very appealing. They say she generally failed in these attempts, for me these very experiments doomed to failure seem interesting. And "The Waves" is a jewel, really. I'm also

interested in the psychological aspect, in the communication beyond language between her characters. V. Woolf is pretty interiorised, which makes her writing more concentrated, shorter and more abrupt.

SA:
I see you are speaking about her in present time.

IN:
Why, do you think of her as dead?

SA:
What other writers, biologically dead, but whom you consider still alive do you like?

IN:
Ha, ha! Your subtle irony is flattering me. Did you know Stuart is the name of a little white mouse with red sneakers and blue short pants on a skateboard?

SA:
Well then, what other writers, biologically dead or not, whom you still think alive do you like?

IN:
Well, after I discovered V. Woolf's books, I logically followed up with T. S. Eliot and James Joyce, Lawrence, Jane Austen and so on. I still avoid Shakespeare for he was much too recommended by all modern writers in their books, he's much too promoted, I also like Fitzgerald and some contemporary Japanese writers whose names are impossible to memorize.

SA:
What is the link between everything you've told me so far about V. Woolf and your favourite

writers and the texts on the coloured cubes in *Monthly Evaluations*? It seems to me there is a resemblance between the auto critical, analytical spirit of V. Woolf and what you do when you select every day certain colours, numbers and words in order to describe the quantity of time in a day.

IN:
Yes, I'm interested in how much you can pin down, in how much you can capture from what is happening every day. In English you have "to cast", a verb with many nuances that explain better what I want to do. Time seems to me quite slippery in everyday life. I wanted to create objects, in fact some cubes to represent time and things that can happen during one day. If I establish some simple rules, a scale and a chromatic table and I decide that everything that happens in a day can be described through these elements—colours, numbers and words—that means I'm able to better observe the phenomenon I want to study. It was difficult at the beginning to draw the chromatic map, to set up the scale from—10 to 0 and +10, but in time I started to readjust them to everyday reality.

SA:
You mean to your subjective reality, or this evaluation grid can be applied to anyone?

IN:
There is a general pattern, but of course every person has his or her own psychic and intellectual system, his or her own evaluation grid. If we made the cube experiment on another person, transforming his or her months in cubes, we would first have to define his/her evaluation grid.

SA:
How much of the *Monthly Evaluations* cubes is autobiography and how much is science?

IN:
How much is art?

SA:
Art seems to me a quite generous term, under its umbrella a lot of oddities can seek shelter. A lot of genetic hybrids, "weird" things that cannot function outside the artistic system. I suppose your experiment too is harboured under this umbrella.

IN:
What I dislike most in this project is the autobiographical part. I confess I hate this kind of art work. But in any experiment you have to refrain yourself from falsifying the numbers, if you want the output to be true.
So I decided that the texts on the cubes must be true. Since they are so short, I'm forced to pay more attention to the words I choose, that's why they look like fiction. Eventually, the same things happen to almost all of us, the most important thing is how you express them.

SA:
And what is the final output? The finished product?

IN:
The cubes. The attempt to create sculpture out of your day, your own time. To measure time and other slippery things such as life itself, emotions or feelings, turning them into other measures: seconds in grams, hours in

kilograms, pulse and ticking in words, depressions and exuberance in colours.

SA:
Have you ever tried to colour your dreams?

IN:
No.

SA:
Why?

IN:
Because dreams are part of another reality, less conscious. I try not to mix things up. Moreover, if I analysed dreams I would have too many unknown elements in this equation and the whole process would appear more like a psychological trick.

SA:
Have you ever looked back to a day and perceived it differently from the way you perceived it initially? Have you marked it as negative in the beginning and then realized it was a positive one?

IN:
In theory it is possible that our perception changes in time, but practically days remain in my memory the way I perceived them initially.

SA:
Do you also deal with memory archiving in your project? Have you thought of archiving your perceptions on one day, any day? That is, by archiving them all, do you offer each day, no matter its intensity, the chance to be remembered?

IN:
Mmm... Interesting question.

SA:
Thank you.

IN:
I never thought of that. At least not of archiving, even though at a certain point I will have gathered an impressive number of days. Or maybe not. I dislike something in the idea of memory that must be kept. Why do so many things have to be kept? I like throwing things away. I think the process of destruction is a very healthy one. We must not give up destruction entirely.

SA:
Why mustn't we?

IN:
Because only after some destruction can giant leaps be made in the evolution of something. Destruction is a very positive thing, it creates new paradigms.

In the background we heard balls bouncing, someone was dribbling around some orange poles, and a girl kept throwing herself to the ground in a weird way, in sort of plunges. We were so absorbed by the discussion that we didn't realize the hall got full with the juniors from CSS5, a local handball club. Before leaving, I asked her what I was supposed to do with the coloured cubes in the magazine and she answered I could do anything I want, but at least I should cut them up and assemble them.

LOCATION: CRÎNGAŞI DAM
SUBJECT: ROMANIAN CONTEXT

This time I was 15 minutes late. Ioana was waiting for me walking up and down on the dam alley. It was not easy for me to trace her for the dam—an artificial lake accumulating the waters of Dîmboviţa; it is a megalomaniac construction, typical of the Ceauşescu era. In the park in front of the dam you feel like a lost Lilliputian in a garden built by and for aliens. Its pattern can be seen only from the air. Neither the park nor the dam were built for ordinary people from the street, but for gods. Ironically, ordinary people have come to populate it, or rather to lose themselves in it. Panting from climbing several hundred format small grey marble stairs, I reached the elevated platform of the dam. The huge lake shines dazzlingly. A strong wind is blowing and the sun feels frosty. Wearing a sort of oversized, light mauve silky nylon vest, gird tightly on the waist with a black plaited leather belt, and a skirt made of two layers, velvety nylon and pale pink satin, quite shiny, which didn't fit the body because of the strange cut, Ioana seems a luminous stripe or a meteorological balloon, giving a general impression of calculated disorder. When I reached her, still panting, I saw that under the short 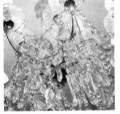 vest she was wearing a pullover with a pattern of deer, squirrels and cones in beige, cappuccino and brown shades. Under the stretched pullover, a bit of a beige wrinkled shirt. General look: fresh and natural, perhaps because of the hair with golden reflexes in the sunlight.

SA:
Why this place?

IN:
It was here that I used to come every morning to jog. It's a very beautiful place, exactly due to the paradoxes it holds. Can you imagine a more natural oasis among these blocks?

SA:
I wouldn't call this natural. Apart from the deserted park and the water from the dam, everything is concrete.

IN:
Come on, don't be fooled by first impressions. The dam unveils itself gradually only if you trust it. Did you know this used to be a cemetery long before? I remember, when I was young, the debates around the dam: whether it was moral to dig out the dead or to simply pour concrete over them. I think they chose a middle solution, digging out what they could and the rest of it remained under the concrete. After they built the dam, there were all kinds of stories about the dead under the concrete asking for their revenge, about pieces of skeletons floating on the water. Anyway, the desire to splash was so strong that there were quite a few people plunging in the lake. Those who drowned were inevitably put on the black revenge list of those under the lake. This was also the place where they found a suitcase full of body parts of a Chinese man. It was all over the news. But apart from that, it looks very scientific, don't you think?

SA:
Scientific?

IN:
Yes, I'm talking about architecture. I like its clean lines, the minimalism of concrete combined with precious

details such as marble stairs, or the amphitheatre pieces on the isle. If you like, we can go on the island, we can get there on foot in half an hour.

> SA:
> OK, let's go. We were supposed to discuss the Romanian context.

IN:
And what do you think is this? Near the island there is a village, or rather an agglomeration of tents. The gipsies leave every morning with their carts to gather and sell scrap iron. They are really skillful, for they can go up and down the steep hill of the dam with their horse and cart. It's a miracle they can do it without turning over, isn't it?

Halfway to the isle I often meet an old and shabby-looking shepherd who grazes his sheep and goats. Can you imagine? He also has a big dog. I find it fascinating to see the grass trying so hard to spring in the middle of the road, to break through the concrete. Just when you take the turn toward the island, a pack of hungry, enraged dogs throw them selves at you, barking. They consume so much energy, climbing this hill, only to bark at you. Don't you think everything around is so Romanian? And we are in a communist neighbourhood only 20 minutes away from the centre.

> SA:
> Yes, it's beautiful. I was speaking about the artistic context.

IN:
Yeah, the artistic one.

On our way we indeed met the urban shepherd who told us he lived in a house scraped up from dung bricks and some cardboard. It's incredible how you can still see something like this nowadays, and I find it all very picturesque and quite romantic. At the turn, the dogs left us alone because fortunately someone had thrown them something to eat. The gipsies already left with their carts. At "home" only children were playing football with a deflated ball, and some older women were carrying out their daily chores in the tents covered with colourful, greasy blankets blackened by so much smoke from the fire made with newspapers and plastic bags.

The small island was nothing but a floating concrete saucer, in the middle of which some wild rose bushes grew. On the edge, the small island was flanked by a fence of willows.

We entered it through a concrete arcade adorned with marble ornaments, probably a copy of a Greek one. The amphitheatre, a sort of terrace with miniature arcades and columns, had some pontoons on one side, from where boats were supposed to sail off.

IN:
Doesn't it all look like a failed scientific project?

[The second row is made up by the following images: a gold chandelier photographed in a warm light, a bullterrier with angels painted on horse skin by G. Fickle that costs 1,500 Euros, two Montblanc fountain pens, limited edition, an "exploded" lamp from the '60s, with cosmic bulbs, a very small photograph with a red curtain in a theatre in ruins, ex Sofia, in Vienna, a portrait of Carolina Herrera with her daughters in a calm August afternoon.

In the background you can hear "Statues" from Moloko's homonym album.]

SA:
Why failed?

IN:
Because it didn't turn out as it was initially planned. Do you see boats or people sitting in the amphitheatre's shade?

SA:
I don't think it's failed since those fishermen on the docks use this space very well. It's true they have rubber tubes from truck tires instead of boats, but still the place is not completely deserted. The saddest place is a deserted one, where not even birds or animals live.

IN:
Once I wanted to make a fictive scientific documentary about this place. It would have been hosted by an Englishman, in white coat, with glasses and a stick, the one that Geography teachers have. Tom is a DJ and he writes quite well in various lifestyle magazines. I would have presented the paradoxes defining this place: the decayed minimalist architecture, with opulent accessories, the ambitious dream of the "architect" dictator on one hand, the miserable condition of polluted water due to carpet washing during weekends, and people inevitably populating it on the other hand. A place with a huge potential, nevertheless in ruins.

SA:
Why didn't you make it?

IN:
The documentary? Maybe because I didn't believe in it as strongly as I should.

SA:
You could have started with some pictures.

IN:
I took some pictures one winter, with a basketball and a writing machine in the snow. Anyway, I hadn't thought of a documentary then, I hadn't yet discovered the sensitive parts of the dam.

SA:
What about now?

IN:
Now, as you know, I have other priorities. Maybe I won't forget it, and one day I'll come back ready to do this documentary. It's sad, isn't it, that everything has its own gestation time, that you can't do it whenever you want, that there is a time and context for everything.

SA:
Waiting doesn't necessarily mean something dreadful. Sometimes waiting has positive effects. What's your view on contemporary Romanian art?

IN:
What's yours?

SA:
I can't really differentiate it from the one in Eastern Europe. In this region amazing changes

happened in the last 15 years. I think it's only natural that after the fall of communism the artists be the first to freely express them selves concerning the political situation, something that was forbidden for so many years. Now only the names of Marina Abramovic', Warhol, who came from Poland, and the IRWIN group cross my mind, but they were not Romanians.

IN:
Well, we have Ion Grigorescu, Dan Perjovschi and subReal.

SA:
I remember, in your emails, you opposed very categorically this East-European trend, of an art debating local or European political problems. Why?

IN:
In general it's good to be preoccupied with the local context in which you live. I don't think it's OK to have only this kind of art, interested only in the political issues, especially those that superficially deal with European issues. I find annoying a lot of young artists who didn't have anything to do with politics and suddenly taking over this subject only because it's trendy. You know how it is, everybody is an expert in football and politics. With a slightly critical approach, a little bit of mockery, a little bit of local colour, some blood, some honey, a few gipsies, not too many, some new media to show we are not that primitive, a bit of design as in advertising, some clubbing and VJing for we already taste the benefits of globalisation, and here you are, a work of pure Romanian contemporary art. In Romania there are very few artists that really have something to say in this niche of political art,

a niche which here is paradoxically represented by the majority. The best example is the recent exhibition held at the opening of MNAC, with artists that loved or didn't love Ceaușescu's palace. How many of the young artists who exhibited then were really interested in *Casa Poporului* before Ruxandra Balaci, the curator, announced to them the subject of the exhibition? How many of them were interested in the subject and how many thought they could not miss such an opportunity to be part of a big international exhibition? Anyway I totally dislike the idea of a commissioned work of art, after a theme given by the curator, it reminds me of the compulsory essays in gymnasium. Have you seen the exhibition?

SA:
I haven't seen even the building yet.

IN:
Well, if you're here, maybe you'll make some time and go to see it. So you'll see the MNAC too.

LOCATION: LIRA CINEMA
SUBJECT: REALITY & FICTION

We went together to the last meeting place. And since I haven't seen *The Eternal Sunshine of the Spotless Mind* with Jim Carrey and Kate Winslet, we decided to go see it together at the Lira movie theatre. We entered a dark passage way through the doors of something that seemed rather to be a local shop[2] and only the unmistakable smell of fresh popcorn made me realize I was

192

2   Where everything is sold, from food to socks and electric home appliances. The local shops, located on the building's ground floors are here before the supermarkets. The new malls represent for these small family businesses a real threat in the next future.

inside a movie theatre. We asked for two movie tickets and the ticket seller who was also the popcorn vendor and the woman tearing up the tickets when entering the cinema hall, looked at us up and down, especially at Ioana. This time she had a bizarre outfit. A black leather skirt, rounded up like a ball, short up to the knee, with a black leather jacket, a doll-like collar and bulging cut, with very big seams that made the entire costume look like a black baseball. We were told we had to wait for some more customers because she wouldn't let the picture begin for only two persons, she would lose money this way. Since we had time to lose and ignoring the fact that maybe no customer would show up and therefore we wouldn't see any movie, we sat down in the dark hallway, on a tiny red leather sofa, with big buttons covered in red leather. Only when seated did I notice that on her head, Ioana had a sort of cover, like those you put on your eyes when you sleep and don't want any light to bother you, made of white satin on which it was written with silvery rhinestones in capital letters, DREAM. All round, the cover was hemstitched with a thin black strap and was fixed on the head with a pale pink lace band. She was wearing it nonchalantly, as if she had just got out of bed. Other strange accessories were the white suede gloves, like those protection gloves worn by motorcycle drivers. I won't even mention the shoes, but they were matching the whole outfit perfectly.

IN:
Can you believe a movie theatre is bankrupt?

> SA:
> This one?

IN:
Yes. It's deserted most of the times, but I like it very much because it is the smallest multiplex cinema I've ever

seen. There are a few rooms, I've only been inside four until now, in which movies are projected simultaneously to maximum 20 people. The smallest room, somewhere in the basement, only has ten seats. Nobody knows how many projection rooms there are in total, but there are a lot of rumours about that, such as if you know the right person you can see prohibited movies.

SA:
You mean porn?

IN:
Not necessarily, you can rent those, isn't it? Homemade movies made by all kinds of individuals crazy about domestic masochism. If there are "directors" like that, why shouldn't there be public for it?

SA:
Have you seen any of these movies?

IN:
No, I only heard there are such movies. Once, late in the night, I was passing by, I saw light and entered. In the hallway, some dubious individuals hurried down the winding stairways, leading to the basement room. The seller was quite disconcerted and told me it was a private audition, that I didn't have an invitation and could not enter. Then I asked for a popcorn bag and she told me she wouldn't sell it to me, because she wanted to bring home the leftovers. That kind of made me feel at home, imagine that this movie theatre could be my home. Let me show you something.

We entered a dark room, not very big but very high. Someone had crammed on several levels some very bulky corner sofas, made of an awful material, grey with blue geometrical patterns. In a discreetly lighted corner, a sort of booth, were some other big armchairs covered in the same horrible cloth. I couldn't help getting closer to observe the pictures on the wall. Framed in glass, there were some of the biggest stars of the cinema, in scenes that became icons in time, such as a dark-haired Uma Thurman in front of a milkshake. The photo was signed with something that seemed the actress's autograph. All the portraits were meticulously and flamboyantly signed in the right down corner. Tens of red and green tiny lights were flickering through the transparent floor of the dancing ring. The walls covered in mirrors took your breath away adding a hallucinatory effect to the whole atmosphere. Right on the dancing ring, near the mirrors, two bulky wooden desks typical of the Ceaușescu era were abandoned. The massive desks reflected in the disco mirrors had a slight pervert air, communist and pervert at the same time.

IN:
It used to be a kind of bar, night club and morning cafe here, but as you can see it didn't hold out and went bankrupt. It's interesting that nobody bothered to replace the decoration, and it stayed on just as it was initially built. You have the feeling you enter a museum hall, mortuary room and worship space all in one, don't you think?

> SA:
> It looks so deserted. As if something suddenly happened and people ran desperately away. I feel like a detective archaeologist.

IN:
It's scary indeed. Let's go.

SA:
I wonder why it went bankrupt?

[On the last row came the following images: a Victorian curtain, made of blue velvet with thin black stripes, a photo with a stranded jelly fish on the shore, clipped from a magazine promoting a British photography contest, an eye cover for sleeping in white satin, and beside it is written, "here is the access ticket to the realm of latent desires", a silvery chain with a silvery coin, silvery key and a golden hen claw hanging from it, from V. Westwood, a mauve and medicinal pink and black shoe, genre Romanian '80s, very sexy, with Apaca-like[3] reminiscences,  from Venera Arapu, published in ELLE, Sept. 2004, the word "interview" on a very small cardboard, written in black permanent marker, and a photocopied sheet of paper with drawings featuring a magpie, an owl and a rose branch. Up on the ceiling, the black shadow of a chandelier is crossed diagonally by two parallel neon lights.]

IN:
I don't know. Maybe it's the location, which is a little isolated, even if close to the centre. It seems that the movieplex is in a sort of clinical death and survives only due to the oxygen pumped by the state. Since they don't have money to buy new films, they make up their program with leftovers from other movie theatres, which are economically healthy. What is not needed anymore is sent to Lira trash bin.

3   Apaca was in communist times a clothing factory that held in Bucharest a monopoly on women clothes industry, providing a unique style, quite dull and uniform. It still exists but produces clothes in lohn system.

SA:
A sort of movie cemetery.

IN:
It's kind of sad when a movie
gets here. After several
weeks it is out of use and it
gets here to take a breath, and then moves forward.

SA:
Forward, where I thought it goes straight to the
garbage.

IN:
I don't think they throw it away. It would be strange
to throw away the film roll, isn't it. Probably it is being
recycled and turned to plastic.

SA:
I don't think so, it's toxic.

IN:
Maybe they burn it in the back of the theatre. It's polluting
either way.

SA:
It would be interesting to follow the trajectory of
a movie, from the writing of the screenplay to the
footage, editing and distribution, from its glorious
era to the total decadence, inside of a garbage bin
in the back of Lira movie theatre.

IN:
All roads lead to Lira!

When finally some lost customers showed up in the doorstep, more exactly two couples, we sprang towards them to ask what movie they were going to. They said something about Angelina Jolie and Alexander and, realizing we were outnumbered and the movie would have been chosen by them, we tried to convince them to go see *The Eternal Sunshine of the Spotless Mind*. If in the beginning Ioana begged them to change their option, now she almost commanded them to see this movie which was better than Alexander, that Alexander's story could be found in any history book and so on and so forth. Unless the ticket seller didn't decide in the last minute, not out of compassion for two patient customers like us who had waited half an hour for the arrival of other customers, but because she had already seen Alexander at home, on a DVD and thought it was stupid, that the six of us would see *The Eternal...*, probably it would have ended with swearing from both sides. And because the projector from room no. 4 had broken, we had to wait for another half hour until they moved the film roll to the basement, in another room. I'll never forget that big and terrifying aluminium wheel, through which you could see the barren denuded film, oil black with green-bluish reflexes. The man from the technical department was simply rolling it in the hallway before our eyes and I felt like I was in a Chinese restaurant where the cook brings before you the snake alive, for you to know what you are going to eat. Before exiting, I reminded Ioana about the initial reason of our meeting, the discussion about reality & fiction.

IN:
What do you think this was?

Some supplementary specifications:

* Stuart Aarsman is not real. He is a fictional character made of several fictive biographies sent to the artist by Falke Pisano, the curator of *Monthly Evaluations* exhibition from Ellen de Bruijne Gallery, Amsterdam. She is currently an MA student at Jan van Eyck Academie, Maastricht. Therefore the interview never took place.

* The translation of the interview was made by Maria Farcaş from Romanian to English.

* The three locations actually exist and are situated in Bucharest. Their description is mostly accurate, with the following exceptions: the sports hall does not have two entrances, for the public and for the sportsmen, but only one long corridor; on the little island there is no marble amphitheatre, no wild roses bushes and no concrete Greek-like arcade at the entrance; as for Lira cinema theatre, there are no stories with forbidden movies and the cinema halls do have more than fifty seats.

* The dam meetings with the old shepherd, the maddened dogs and gipsy children are all real. In Lira movie theatre, the waiting for more clients, the negotiations to see the preferred movie and the transport of the film role through the cinema hall by the technical man are actually true.

* During the interview the artist was dressed with clothes inspired by the following fashion collections: As Four, Fall 2005 in the sports hall, Stella McCartney, Winter 2004 on the Crîngaşi dam and Rei Kawakubo, Comme des Garçons, Spring 2005 in Lira cinema theatre.

* The two questions that Stuart addressed to the artist, if she ever thought of evaluating dreams and if perception doesn't change in time, where actually addressed by Julia van Mourik, ex-executive editor at RE- magazine, and one of the organizers of Lost & Found evenings in Amsterdam. These events try to present the artists and their works in a more casual & friendlier atmosphere.

* The wall and the pictures glued on it that appear inserted in the interview are real and located in the artist's studio.

* The black shadow of the chandelier diagonally crossed by the parallel neon lights is not located in the artist's studio but in add office, a non-profit organisation specialized in cultural marketing, and the shadow is an intervention of the artist in this space, located in Bucharest.

* The copyright of all photos in the interview belong entirely to their authors.

* The structure and form of the interview took inspiration from RE- a magazine about one person, especially no. 9 about John and no. 10 about Claudia.

* The interview was written by Ioana Nemeş.

Geir Haraldseth

is a curator based in Oslo, Norway.

He is currently co-curating a survey show of the contemporary art scene in Norway, which is the inaugural exhibition for the new National Museum building in Norway opening in 2021. In 2022 he will co-curate the Dutch Pavilion at the Venice Biennale featuring the work of Melanie Bonajo.

Previous positions include director of Rogaland Kunstsenter (NO), where he initiated an experimental summer school program and a library, and curator at the Academy of Fine Arts in Oslo.

Haraldseth holds a BA in Fine Arts from Central Saint Martin's College of Art and Design and an MA in Curatorial Studies from Bard College.

Haraldseth has contributed to several journals and magazines including Art in America, the Exhibitionist, Kunstkritikk, Acne Paper, and Landings Journal.

His work as an independent curator focuses on the links between art and the luxury goods market and he has curated shows at GucciVuitton, Miami (US), Vox Populi, Philadelphia (US), Fotogalleriet, Oslo (NO), Landings Project Space, Vestfossen (NO), the National Museum of Art, Design and Architecture, Oslo (NO), Stavanger Kunstmuseum, Stavanger (NO), Teatro de Arena, São Paulo (BR), and Akershus Kunstsenter, Lillestrøm (NO).

Curatorial residencies awarded include Futura, Prague (CZ); ISCP, New York (US); Capacete, Rio de Janeiro (BR); and Parse, New Orleans (US).

NEOCLASSICAL

A friend of mine, who was living in the 'loca' city of Miami for a few years, joked that her temporary home by the sea was constructed out of chewing gum. When someone mentions Miami it is usually the wonderful Art Deco buildings of South Beach that pop to mind. The city first appeared to me at a young age through the skewed lens of the sleazy and grimy American police drama Miami Vice, and the buildings had the colour palette of subdued chewing gum: dull neon pinks, chewed-out greens, or just dirty yellows. The comment didn't just cover the colours, but extended to considering chewing gum as the actual building material of the city. This rang true, as the existence of the hotels, cafes and residential buildings seemed precarious, as if built by straw or sticks, or gum; and that any fortification and mending of a building could be done using methods like chewing on a piece of gum and patching up whichever surface was missing.

Being a jet-setting, professional flâneur, judging cities across the world with only a fine art education and a large quantity of pop cultural knowledge, I was thinking about bubble gum when I first arrived in Bucharest. However not related to the stories I had read about the currency of chewing gum in Romania. The newspaper articles stated that Romanian gangs would steal packets of chewing gum from stores in the United Kingdom to bring back to Romania as looted gold. I do not know the value of contemporary gum, but it was not used as a construction material. Bucharest did not remind me of South Beach in any way, but I wondered: "What is this city made of?"

Bucharest, as most cities, reveals part of its history and power dynamics through architecture. There are beautiful buildings of many different styles, and the city bears apparent marks of push and pull expansion and different expressions of power. The mass housing estates from the communist era are meticulously planned out to offer no hope of green parks or of individual

204

excess, while other areas seem more haphazard and accidental, and not to mention occidental, prone to anachronistic advances and personal gestures.

The extravagant Neoclassical and eclectic Second Empire styles lead me through the city to the more functional and modern projects. I could see why the city was called Little Paris, seeing as not just the buildings gave me an air of Paris, but there were also similar amounts of dog-poop on the streets. I could also swap the name Bucharest for Ceaușescuville, because the dirty dictator left so many visible marks on the city. The Neoclassical, or at least the imaginary of Neoclassicism, must have meant something very special to Nicolae Ceaușescu. He erected a wet dream of Neoclassical spectres and ordered the destruction of seven square kilometres of the old city to make room for the Palatul Parlamentului. This meant that several blocks of the capital, including Uranus Hill, residential buildings, public buildings and monasteries were erased, and 40,000 people were forcibly moved. The Palace of the Parliament and its surroundings are immense. If you have ever been to Bucharest, you'll know how hard it is to miss this area. You can probably see it from the moon. The Palace itself is one of the largest buildings in the world with a volume of 2.55 million m^3.

During my first visit to Bucharest, for a seminar on European archives in the contemporary art field, most of the meetings took place at the National Museum of Contemporary Art of Romania. The museum was given a small space in the palace, as the building always has too much room and not enough filling. Only a small percentage of the building is in use to this day. No wonder it took me a while to find the entrance to the museum, as walking around the structure takes a while, all the time trying to find a way which wasn't blocked by angry looking guards. I tried my hardest not to be harassed by the guards that were actively seeking subjects to look suspiciously at.

I joined a tour of the building to see more than just the minuscule museum of contemporary art. On the tour the building itself was coming apart in front of my eyes. I must have blinked out on to one of the balconies, but I could practically see the materials of the building erode away. The Neoclassical surfaces revealed their inner construction, iron supports jutting out of the poor stones. Bits of stone were falling off, as if the glue had worn out. This was not chewing gum. I would maybe say sand castles, as the impossibility of the building was apparent and it would take only one wave to wash away the forms and leave a husk of a structure behind. Order and reason were main concerns of the Neoclassic style. It stood in stark contrast to the sluttyness of Rococo. The grandeur and scale of Neoclassical architecture might be what appealed to Ceaușescu, not necessarily its ties to the age of Enlightenment.

With the privilege of hindsight Ceaușescuville stands out. It stands out amongst its similar siblings in other Eastern European dictatorships, or even among the Pyongyangs of the world. It stands out as the only Neoclassicist city transformation on a large scale in the last few decades, maybe only matched by the recreation of copycat European cities forming in China. The value of the Neoclassicist as the epitome of European ideals seems the desirable object, but as a sandcastle in a world that is falling apart morally and environmentally, it is a mere folly. Something that gets chewed up and spat out.

Jimmy Robert

(b.1975 in Guadeloupe, FR) lives and works in Berlin.

Jimmy Robert works with diverse media including photography, collages, objects, art books, short films and performance art. Questions of identity and its representation are his main interest, and he uses a variety of references from literature, art and music to emphasise the fragility of the materials he uses. In some performances Robert's body becomes a projection surface, where the tension between the portrayal and the content reveal the relationship between appropriation and alienation. In previous works, Robert has explored the politics of spectatorship by reworking seminal avant-garde performances in ways that complicate their racial and gendered readings.

In recent years, Robert has exhibited at 8th Berlin Biennale of Contemporary Art, Berlin (DE), Tate Britain, London (UK), WIELS, Brussels (BE), CCA Kitakiushu Project Gallery (JP), Chicago Architecture Biennial (US), Cubitt Gallery, London (UK), Neuer Aachen Kunstverein (DE), CAC Bretigny (DE) and performed at MoMA New York (US), Performa 17 (US), KW, Berlin (DE).

Solo shows at Jeu de Paume, Paris (FR), MCA Chicago (US), Power Plant, Toronto (CA).

A touring mid-career survey of the practice of Jimmy Robert started recently at Nottingham Contemporary (UK) and will be followed by shows at CRAC de Sète (FR) and Museion Bolzano (IT).

He is currently professor of Sculpture and Performance at Universität der Künste – UdK, Berlin.

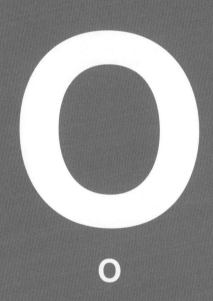

O

Her story has been told many times, under pseudonyms, by women, by men passing as women, in films, in comics. So she took over the name with no hesitation and set up her own business in downtown Bucharest City in one of those lush Art Deco buildings left over by the second communist revolution.

She had started a network of video chat mostly employing over qualified young women straight out of university, the kind of really smart foxy PhD students who needed to make ends meet, who could generate thousands of Dollars just by entertaining lonely Scandinavian women who could afford the high rate but couldn't tolerate the isolation of the high career jobs now available only in the North of Europe during those long Summers inherited from climate change.

Feminism had undergone yet another backlash and men were reclaiming their rights to watch endless football matches together and drink beer and burp loudly while scratching their balls in fraternity. No one else was invited.

The set up for the online dating was extraordinary. One could choose a décor, characters as well as costumes; very much like those video games of the 21st century except that now the augmented reality allowed more intimacy with her staff, one was in the room with the girls, almost in a domestic relationship, for a moderate fee.

O had learnt the hard way, having sold parts of her body to the black market, she knew all too well what love meant and what giving yourself entirely, body and soul, meant, neither ghost, nor shell, but a perfect synthesis of algorithmic desires. She knew what all wanted before they even dreamt of asking.

Perfection had a price and it was black gold. After China had taken over the last oil plants of Nigeria and endless fracking had rendered the soil sterile, most of the population had fled to the uninhabited regions of the East of Europe where she was now ruling as the Queen of the Night. Or was it the Queen of Hearts?

She roamed the dark streets in her long luxurious car; they were still lighted with this yellow light of the old times and from her tinted windows could reminisce the uneven beauty of each building and how the city blossomed at night. The perfect simulacrum of Parisian boulevards, the sexual night, the one of novels, the one of sacrifices of innocence, innocence... that word sounded familiar as it came up, like sweet flowers in the summer kidnapping the senses and burgeoning at her infrared lips, obliterating the nerves.

The windows of the imported car went up automatically, there was no more time for nostalgia as business had to be done, time was money, old saying from old movies but she needed to make sure that she was not outsmarted by one of these emerging savvy and ambitious younger girls, who had read the novel too, knew the streets story just as well and would not let any opportunity pass them by.

The car swiftly drove by the ruins of an orthodox church, the last vestige of a cruising ground of the ever-growing trans population. She recognised it as she had lost her virginity there a long time ago when she was still organic.

Something had to be said about the way the technology of touch had evolved in Bucharest city, BC as they called it. Where 4D porn was the most flourishing venture. I guess by now you could call her Madame O. Her house and her girls were renowned. She had earned her respect at all levels of society, she owned shares, controlled markets and owned most politicians, adored and yet feared she had raised this beautiful green eyed Roma boy, one of the last (I had personally only heard of him through tales) to one day replace her at the head of her empire.

O distinguished herself by her interiors too, she had learned to transform the eroticism of Memphis into a reality, her sofas would make love to you, the colours were vibrating, the materials were electrifying and orgasmic. She had taste and no one could take that away from her, even after they had allegedly stripped her of her humanity. Virtually, of course.

Lea Rasovszky

(b. 1986, Bucharest) is interested in marginal cultural subjects, from areas such as kitsch, *manele*, social underdogs, non-conforming bodies and individuals, and "psychological peripheries" that are not purely social. Her artworks are, most often, portraits in motion of people, situations, and emotions filtered through an ironic and rough drawing style paired with installations that highlight the stereotypes and values of the society towards which she has a critical view.

Selected shows: *BRUIAJ*, Art Encounters Foundation, Timișoara (RO), *EX-EAST Past and Recent Stories of the Romanian Avant-gardes*, Espace Niemeyer, Paris (FR), *Homo Deus*, Mobius Gallery, New York (US), *I Am At My Most Beautiful When I Am Alone*, Mobius Gallery, Bucharest (RO), *Four Drawings and a Book*, White Cuib, Cluj-Napoca (RO), *Life a User's Manual: Who's Afraid of Politics?*, Art Encounters II edition, Timișoara, (RO), *DADA GAMES*, Rumänisches Kulturinstitut Berlin, Berlin (DE), *FLIRT*, Im Hinterzimmer, Karlsruhe (DE), *Building Modern Bodies*, Kunsthalle Zürich (CH), *Inventing the Truth. On Fiction and Reality*, The New Gallery of the Romanian Institute for Culture and Humanistic Research in Venice, 56th edition of the Venice Art Biennial 2015 (IT), *PASAJ*, The National Museum of Contemporary Art – Anexa, Bucharest (RO), *From Stars to Steroids: Two Short Stories About an Almost Metaphoric Bestiary*, Anca Poterașu Gallery, Bucharest (RO); *Inner Whimp*, Lateral ArtSpace, Paintbrush Factory, Cluj-Napoca (RO); The Biennial of Young Artists, 5th edition, Overlapping Biennial, Bucharest (RO).

🌐 https://learasovszky.com

PERIPHERY

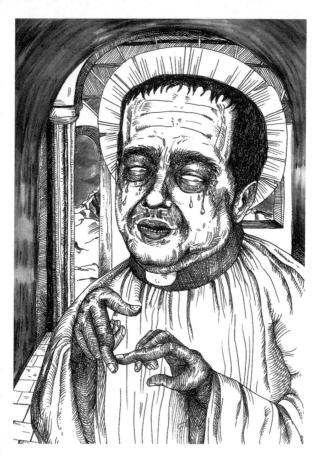

Did you know they used to paint the faces of the poor and improper, on the bodies of saints? They were the only ones whose stillness could be bought. This secret gesture of mischief but also of convenience allowed their realness to be hung high in churches as images of Immaculate Divinity. Kings and queens prayed to them,

The Devil is an ugly crier

not knowing they were bowing their heavy golden heads and praying all their wishes of heaven and wealth to humanity at its most vulnerable and raw.
Reality smells like heavy sweat, struggles and hot skin and no one ever dreams to achieve it.
Yet it is the holiest of representations for it is Life itself.

219

*Did you know my body is flower?
I cultivate its singularity like I
would a garden, I pour only the
sweetest dew into it, I feed it fruit
peels and glittery steroid parti-
cles and I mold it into something
supreme, like you've never seen
before. I slave over making it mon-
umental and godlike and hiding
all hints of frailty. They would
totally spoil my carefully thought
out flora.*

*That (Frailty, the other terrible F
word) is only for me to know, right
before I fall asleep when there's no
stopping these thoughts, letting
my weight sink deep into the softness of my bed, wishing I was it,
knowing I am it.*

221

I feel only the thumping in my ears and vibrations on the souls of my feet. They move upwards in my entire body and I can almost feel my blood vessels protruding and drawing on my skin as blood rushes do define them.
I have left my human self and am now something else, something I refuse to define.

I don't need sunlight, I don't work like that. I thrive in closed spaces where the air is heavy and stale and it furthers me into this trance that my body knows so well. It is a ritual that strips me down to an essence that needs no words, just primal instinct and pure violence blooming out of my chest like a carnivorous rose.

224

A stranger giving you a smile for free.

Creepy, am I right?

Why?

Karol Radziszewski

(b. 1980) lives and works in Warsaw (Poland), where he received his MFA from the Academy of Fine Arts in 2004.

He works with film, photography, installations and creates interdisciplinary projects.

His archive-based methodology crosses multiple cultural, historical, religious, social and gender references. Since 2005 he has been the publisher and editor-in-chief of DIK Fagazine. He is the founder of the Queer Archives Institute (2015).

His work has been presented in institutions such as the Museum of Modern Art (US), Zachęta National Gallery of Art, Warsaw (PL), Whitechapel Gallery, London (UK), Kunsthalle Wien (AT), New Museum, New York (US), VideoBrasil, São Paulo (BR), TOP Museum, Tokyo (JP), Kunsthaus Graz (AT), Cobra Museum, Amsterdam (NL), Wrocław Contemporary Museum (PL), Museum of Contemporary Art, Krakow (PL) and Muzeum Sztuki, Łódź (PL). He has participated in several international biennales including PERFORMA 13, New York (US), 7th Göteborg Biennial (SE), 4th Prague Biennial (CZ) and 15th WRO Media Art Biennale (PL).

🌐 http://www.karolradziszewski.com

QUEER

DIK FAGAZINE

FOUNDED IN 2005
WWW.DIKFAGAZINE.COM

I visited Romania first time in July 2007 and returned with my partner Pawel Kubara in November to continue the research for "DIK Fagazine" in Bucharest.

In searching for queerness in Romanian masculinity we conducted several intimate and personal interviews that became a real document of time.

~~In most of the post soci~~

In most of the post-socialist countries oral histories are the dominant type of "documents" testifying to queer history. Compared with Poland, the Romania LGBT history is a story of real absence. Same-sex relationships were criminalized here between the Middle Ages and __2001.__ !!!

Every material trace of a non-heterosexual nature, be it photo, letter, or a story, was seen as evidence of crime.

DIK FAGAZINE No.7 "ROMANIA" ISSUE was launched in Bucharest in 2008 at a crowded ~~str~~ queer party hosted by the artist-run space Kunsthalle Batistei (a garage in the city center)

DAN PERJOVSCHI: "If you participate in a gay parade in Bucharest you will not get beaten as in Moscow. But not many people will dance with you"

PAUL DUNCA: "It's really great to be here at the moment when everything is just blooming.

RIGHTS

DE~~A~~TH TO GAYS

"Romania wants to become part of Europe, not of Sodom" — Bartolomeu Anania (bishop of Transylvania)

QUEENS

"QUEENS" - the first gay club in Bucharest.
Founded in 2002 and opened in this location
in 2006.
ISSA NEBAL - owner and the real Queen
of this place
- moved from Syria
to Bucharest in 1991

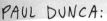

PAUL DUNCA:

"I feel like if there will be a documentary movie about this generation I will be the **gay guy** from the generation"

✳

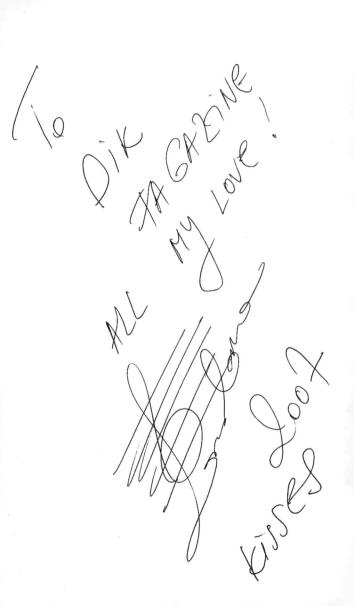

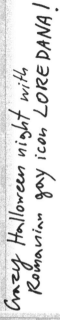

Crazy Halloween night with Romanian gay icon LORE DANA!

1.11. 2007

BUKARESZT

◀ kino „DACIA"
   Calea Grivitei 137

◀ kino „TIMPURI NOI"
   Bulevardul Gheorghiu Dej 18.

○ Canul cu bere   str. Stavropoleos 5

○ café „Athenée Palace"   hotelowa
   str. Episcopiei 1-3

○ café „Union"   hotelowa.
   str. 13 Decembrie 11-13

▤ basen w hotelu „Lido".
   Bulevardul Magheru 5-7

   Bar Magheru   (B L M)?

o.c.
— Calea Victoriei

— Bulevardul Magheru

— Bulevardul Gheorghiu Dej
   park Cişmigiu.

A year after I published DIK Fagazine "Romania" issue
I met Ryszard Kisiel.

At the beginning of the 1980s, Kisiel, the future
initiator and editor of "Filo", one of the first
queer zines in Central and ~~Eastern~~ Eastern
Europe embarked on a range of journeys
around Poland and abroad. Traveling with
his camera by trains he visited Hungary,
* Czechoslovakia, Bulgaria, GDR and
ROMANIA.

His interests focused on bars, bathhouses, parks,
toilets – cruising places where homosexuals
met in the 1970s and 1980s.

He visited Bucharest for the first time
in 1975.

"Polish Gay Guide on the Europeans Socialists
Countries" is more then 300 pages notebook
that he was gradually completing
while traveling.

Ștefan Botez

(b. 1983 in Bucharest, RO) studied architecture in Bucharest and visual arts in Geneva, where he lives and works. His passion for cinema is visible throughout his video work, but also in his installations, performances and drawings where past, present and future don't seem to succeed one another, but rather to be part of the same space-time continuum. And so, his work, a reflection on aesthetics of masculinity, becomes more ambiguous and profound.

Nominated for the Platform 15 Award, Geneva (CH), 2014 and winner of the Open Frame Award Go EAST, Deutsches Filminstitut & Filmmuseum, Frankfurt (DE), 2014, his work was shown at: MNAC (RO), MAFA, Arad (RO), Kunstraum Walcheturm, Zürich (CH), Maison des Arts de Grütli, Geneva (CH), Video deli #1, Paris (FR), Palazzetto Bru Zane, Venice (IT), The Art Encounters Biennial, Timișoara (RO), Eastwards Prospectus, Bucharest (RO), MAMCO, Geneva (CH), Hebbel Am Ufer, Berlin (DE), Milkshake Agency, Geneva (CH), Nassauischer Kunstverein, Wiesbaden (DE), An Lanntair Arts Center, Isle of Lewis (UK), The Brukenthal National Museum, Sibiu (RO).

His work was published in print and online in publications such as: The New York Times, Mousse Magazine, The Rest is Noise and various exhibition catalogues.

🌐 https://stefanbotez.tumblr.com

RESILIENCE

A tenacious weed, in rich cities the Tree of Heaven is being finished off, while in cities with less radiant economies such as Berlin, Detroit, Bucharest, etc. the plant is left to flourish. The tree grows unbothered amidst melancholic ruins of a still too present past, earning thus its moniker of **Ghetto Palm**.

These landscapes of Bucharest come to the artist's mind as a long-forgotten dream and the Tree of Heaven becomes for Ștefan Botez the symbol of his town, his place of birth. At the beginning of his voluntary exile to Geneva, the artist created this series of drawings, which started with the sketched frailty of a bud, ending in the flamboyant foliage of a full-grown tree.

Through these solitary trees, with no roots and no ground—that float in the white of the drawing paper—the artist produces a self-portrait. The Tree of Heaven is Bucharest and it is him. Him in his displacement where he finds the other, but especially himself. Him, the foreigner finding his way, fractured, who says 'I' as this tree says 'I'. I live, I grow! I am the Tree of Heaven, I am the foreigner, the undesirable, with my wrinkled foliage, my broken, worthless timber, my cat urine stinking sap.

— Julie Gil

Simina Neagu

(b. 1988, Bucharest, RO) is an arts administrator, curator and writer based in London, currently working as Assistant Curator / Programme and Operations Coordinator at Iniva (Institute of International Visual Arts).

She holds an MA in Aesthetics and Art Theory from Centre for Research in Modern European Philosophy, Kingston University London and is currently part of the programme CuratorLab 2020/2021 at Konstfack University, Stockholm. She is a member of SHERA (Society of Historians of East European, Eurasian, and Russian Art and Architecture).

Her research-based and interdisciplinary practice, often in collaboration with curator Valentina Bin, facilitates critical reflection, community building and collective learning through public programming and publishing. Her projects often explore questions of political agency, access, labour and diasporic narratives.

She has previously worked with various arts organisations including Gothenburg Museum of Art (SE), Chisenhale Gallery, London (UK), CCA Ujazdowski Castle Warsaw (PL), Bucharest Biennale (RO), Project Biennial of Contemporary Art D-0 ARK Underground (BA), as well as an assistant for artists such as Céline Condorelli, Aleksandra Mir and Rana Begum.

Her writing was published in Springerin, Revista ARTA, and Kajet Journal, amongst others.

🌐 https://www.siminaneagu.com

S

STRAYING

Dear Mărgica,

I remember how they brought you home in a textile bag we used to carry potatoes in. You were born in April 2000. I remember those times as buoyant glimmers, of slowly returning enthusiasm and bad Swiss franc mortgages. There were new cars on the streets of Bucharest. The previous summer, we sat on the balcony watching the total solar eclipse of 1999. I remember looking at the dark halo of the sun through the plastic window of a specially issued bank note, in anticipation of a new age, which you ushered in. You were three months old and the concrete walls were hot the night you arrived. Sniffing around the flat, you stopped on the balcony. A street called the Field of Freedom stretched beyond the estate. Labour Square stood to the West, Iancului Square to the East. Between them, Mihai Bravu Street connected point A to point B. That would become your domain, your field of freedom and it was between those two metro stops that you spent most of your life. Your day-to-day had the simplest geometry.

I'd like to imagine us going for a walk or maybe taking the tram. I'd like to imagine us straying from your usual territory, from our well-trodden paths between the two stations, weaving behind the church and police station and avoiding the cemetery. I was always too scared to take you there. Not just because of the stray dogs that were hostile to you, but the ghosts dwelling there, your grandparents amongst others. Animal ghosts mingled with them too. There were pigs, chickens and horses that lived and died before you in this drained swamp that we now call our neighbourhood. Water was pumped out of the soil and new, stout houses were built as a continuation of the Malaxa factories. Soon enough, the animals moved further and further away to the border of the city. Out, out, with any traces to remind us that we were once neighbours. But your cousins stayed behind. Behind every council estate, behind every shop, stadium, restaurant and school was a "wasteland dog", "community dog", "pariah dog", refusing to be sanitised and packed away in a cage. The smell of urban chickens and pigs slowly faded from memory, but the smell of muddy, wet dog lingered on: a petrichor particular to Bucharest.

You look at me with your beady eyes and almost say: "You're trying to copy Eileen Myles." And you are right. I had them sign a copy of their book *Afterglow. A Dog Memoir* in your name, just before your eighteenth birthday. Eileen wrote this after their dog Rosie died. During the reading I kept thinking of you, the obsessive thought of coping with your death kept circling. Eileen was signing books outside and I didn't have any cash on me. My friend Iulia lent me £10 and I rushed to the front and muttered to Eileen: "Can you make it to my dog?" I spelled your name slowly M-Ă-R-G-I-C-A and Eileen obliged. I didn't open it for two years. Too many ghosts between the pages of one book.

I'm already straying, but what I'm departing from on our walk is more *The Irony of the Leash* than *Afterglow*. Now that you are a ghost too, we can stroll without a leash. You find this ironic. I tell you not all asymmetrical relations are unethical. You blink in disbelief. You tell me you always hated wearing a collar and the harness was uncomfortable too; I guess ethics implies a shared language. I ask you if we didn't share a language. "Of course we did." You say, shaking your ears. "But you chose to ignore my discomfort."

Should we take the tram? The steps are high and I would have had to lift you up in my arms, but now you're so light. As I hold onto the slightly greasy pole I wonder if you're all angry with us. You know what I mean. The indentured emotional labour, arranged marriages, forced sterilisations, etc. ... One day we will have to pay

this debt. Eileen knew this when they imagined getting a letter from Rosie's lawyer. You remind me that you never signed a contract. Food in exchange of emotional intimacy, did that work out for you? I try to distract your attention. I point to a stray dog sitting on a chair, looking out the window. You remind me it's well documented that stray dogs use the metro system in Moscow. They get on and off at specific stops, they avoid the rush hour. The stray turns around, studies us, and unbothered, rolls into the shape of a pretzel. The tracks make a repetitive clanging sound, an industrial lullaby.

You remind me how rare this sight has become. Several waves of ecocide between 2000 and 2015 have wiped out almost the entirety of Bucharest's stray dog population. You say ecocide but what you actually mean is genocide. "Can you say it with the same force?" you ask me. I don't know if I can and you're disappointed with me. You remind me of Article 8 in the Universal Declaration of Animal Rights from 1978, then revised in 1989: "Any act compromising the survival of a wild species and any decision leading to such an act are tantamount to genocide, that is to say, a crime against the species." I wonder how you learned all of this and want to pet your head and say: "Your English is so good." I stop myself just at the right time.

"There are no memorials, no statues, no plaques to commemorate what happened." You continue and remind me of the story of Malchik, the stray metro dog of Moscow, who got his own statue at Mendeleyevskaya station after being killed by a commuter in 2001. They named the statue *Compassion*, celebrating relationships with homeless animals. A bronze Malchik sits on top of a bronze blanket and looks up, in pure surprise, perhaps seconds before being attacked. You want the same for your cousins and I understand, but there's no singular place where the murders occurred. And how can there be a memorial when their ghosts are still here? You some-times see them in the flash of a car, behind a trashcan, at the corners of buildings. The corners are always restless in this city. The dogs are weaving in and out, between the legs of commuters at Victoriei Square. They take the first metro, usually on the M1 line and wander through the city. Commemoration is the first step towards forgetting. Leave them sleepless, let them haunt and stray, deliver-ing small ghost-bites at the ankles of commuters. The living and un-living spill out of their assigned edges, colouring the city outside the lines.

As the no. 10 tram goes past Wind Street, your tail starts wagging. You've never been to this part of the city, except maybe in a car. Your eyes dart across the opaque waters of Dâmbovița. A lone fish blows bubbles close to the surface, relieved the fishermen have given up and packed their gear. The stray dog, let's call him Bosquito, turns in the opposite direction. A muddy feeling of pity mixed with guilt overwhelms me. You've never really wandered through your city, stuck between the two stops. Were you happy, endlessly marking your territory at the same designated spots? I don't ask you but I know you can read my mind. You look at Bosquito, whose fur still bears the marks of a distant puddle-bath. He would travel across town every day, sometimes beyond the borders of the city. He had smelt the many edges of things, of benches, of pavements, of shoes, of dandelions. With one lateral sniff he could smell the edges of sadness too.

Suddenly, Bosquito gets up, all stiff and tense and rushes to the door. You signal we should follow him. Non-descript blocks to the left, non-descript blocks to the right, with a Lidl in the middle. His ears pricked up, Bosquito follows a long backstreet and dashes between the cars. A wide field stretches beyond the parking lot and a narrow path cuts through the wild grass. We ended up in Văcărești, the wild wetland of Southern Bucharest. Văcărești, part of a failed urban water infrastructure project meant to connect the city with the Danube river, was abandoned in 1989. The waters never merged and reeds overran the concrete. Herons moved in, weasels, foxes, even turtles and otters. Bosquito rushes deeper into the wetland and we try to keep up. Despite your short legs, it's easier for you than it is for me, as usual. There's nothing but wild grass as far as I can see. You turn around and demand me to hurry up. Your impatience is still there, across time and space, right next to the core of who you are. Bosquito, the muddy-grey flâneur, stops on a concrete platform and waits. Slowly, other stray dogs trickle in and join him. There are tall, short-haired ones, the colour of polished brass and short black ones, with honey-coloured eyes. Some are preoccupied and apprehensive, keeping an eye on a group of people in the distance, while others lounge on the concrete platform watching the red herons fish. These are their last few days in Văcărești, before they embark on their seasonal migration to the South, thousands of kilometers away. The winds have started to change and they will soon be on their way, flying over Bulgaria, Greece, the Mediterranean Sea and then down to Libya. A scattering of brown and yellow eyes follows their every move with reverence. They have travelled further and wider than any of these dogs ever will. It's early September and the sun's lowering path coats the distant tower blocks in an amber film. For a few seconds, the wetlands are still. Is this where all the ghosts come to rest? You roll into a pretzel and all that muted grief washes over. You want to stay with them and study the city in ways you could never do before. Simply with the technology of your nose and the softness of your paws. One of the dogs drops a piece of bread and any other day, you'd be rushing to catch it and hide it behind your teeth. No matter how many times you'd be fed, you'd still fear that each one was your last meal. Did you trust us to come back, in this repetitive ritual of warming up your food and filling up your bowl? But not now, you're motionless and unfazed. You look at the dog, heaving over his piece of wet bread and there's little jealousy in your eyes. "They were crumbs anyway." You seem to say. "All that for a few crumbs."

Bogdan Iancu

holds a PhD in Anthropology and Ethnology (2011) from the University of Perugia (Italy) and an MA in Anthropology (2003) from the National University of Political Studies and Public Administration (Bucharest).

For the last fifteen years he has worked as a researcher based at the National School of Political Studies and Public Administration (Department of Sociology) and the Museum of the Romanian Peasant Bucharest (Department of Ethnological Research), conducting long- and short-term ethnographic researches.

As Assistant Professor of Anthropology, he is teaching Ethnography and Participant Observation, Visual Anthropology, Sociology of Everyday Life, Anthropology of Work.

His research interests focus on housing and material culture, technology and consumption, urban environment, agriculture and agricultural policies. A selection of titles of the articles and chapters he has published include, among others: "Ethnographic and Observational Turn in Contemporary Roma Representations" in *Romanian Cinema Inside Out: Insights on Film Culture, Industry and Politics 1912-2019* (ed. Irina Trocan, Romanian Cultural Institute, 2019), "Landscape, adjective" (co-author) in *Borrowed Territories* (ed. Lucian Bran - Galeria Posibilă, 2016), "Keywords of Romanian Post-Communism" in *RO_Archive. An Archive of Romania in Times of Transition* (ed. Iosif Kiraly et al. - UNArte Publishing House & Vellant, 2015), "The Károly Kós Experiment: Participatory Museography, Material Culture and Childhood" in Martor Review (No 18, 2013), "The Golden Age of the Termopan. The Social Life of Post-socialist Windows", în Martor Review, 16 / 2011.

TRESPASSING

During the 2000s in Romania, as in the other post-socialist countries, changes to the urban landscapes have been particularly conspicuous. As several studies indicated, the most visible element of these "rejuvenations" seems to be the domestic environment. In the housing landscape, the replacement of the classic wooden-framed by double glazed windows and the enclosure of the balcony was one of the strongest statements on taste and change. But it is also regarded by state and marketing discourses as a taken-for-granted panacea for energy saving.

TERMOPANE AS VERNACULAR DISCOURSE

In the last decade in most cases when somebody was buying a flat, the first step of its renovation[1] began (and sometimes ended as well) with the *termopan* window: then a similar step was taken for closing off the balcony, which used to be a common practice in socialist Romania (Poenaru, 2008) related to precarious housing conditions. In Ceaușescu's Romania the enclosure of the balcony was illegal. However despite the harsh fines, many people ignored the law and enclosed their balconies anyway. Twenty years after the '89 revolution the domestic material culture integrated the double-glazed windows (*termopane* in Romanian) with such enthusiasm that it has already led to the occurrence of some lexical derivatives regarding specific "architectural theatricalization" (Manning, 2008), materiality: *termopanizare* (double-glazification in English), *termopanitate* (double-glazity in English).

1   Immediate renovation is a matter of course when speaking about a flat in a "socialist" building.

THE CONSTRUCTION OF THE NEED FOR THERMAL INSULATION

As in other Eastern-European countries the double-glazed industry has also been encouraged in the last few years (starting from 2007) by the authorities based on the use of EU Structural Funds, who wanted to "help" apartment owners to reduce heat losses caused by previous precarious building. The extensive scale of district heating (DH) networks existing in the post-socialist states of Eastern and Central Europe (ECE) is considered by Poputoaia and Bouzarovski (2009) as an implementation tool for the political ideologies and development policies of socialist states.

Like the infrastructure, the block undoubtedly lent itself to a number of specific ideological projects on the part of the State. In light of the country's accession to the EU a national strategy for saving energy politics was designed, especially focusing on the thermal rehabilitation of blocks of flats. Therefore, in the last ten years, the urban landscape of Bucharest often resembled that of a city after an earthquake or a bombardment: hundreds of construction sites cover the districts, and old windows are taken down and left for a while leaning against the fences surrounding the buildings.

SHAPING CONTRASTS AND ANXIETIES

The residential experience in insulated apartments becomes the desired standard for most people, therefore generating anxieties for those who, for some reason, were excluded and are self-defined as "second rank citizens". It is not only a matter of deprivation of access to revitalised infrastructure—by means of *termopane* and polystyrene—but also one of captivity in a grey horizon, associated with the precariousness of socialism.

In addition, at the end of the insulation process there lies another prize for the residents: the certificate of energetic performance of their buildings and apartments. Since 2013 no apartment can be sold without this certificate.

VOICES FROM THE REHABILITATION OFFICE DESK (BUCHAREST)

*) Mrs. Laura bought an apartment in a building erected at the beginning of the 1980s. Some of the accessories that caught her attention and played a fundamental part in the purchase decision were the exterior wooden blinds on the apartment's windows. Two months later, the building entered the insulation process. The construction workers removed the wooden blinds in order to cover the window frames with polystyrene. When asked repeatedly

to reinstall the blinds, the workers told her that it was technically impossible because they were not trained for such operations.

I met Mrs. Laura in the waiting room of the municipal office for thermal insulation of District 1 of Bucharest. She was distressed for not having managed to identify a solution to the problem created by the workers' intervention.[2] The municipality clerk listened calmly but without seeming to empathise in any way, then lifted his shoulders: "there is nothing we can do." But Mrs. L. did not resign: "I will make a criminal complaint for destruction against the company in charge of the building's insulation! What has become of us, are we back to communism when they could destroy[3] our things when they felt like it?"[4]

*) It was at the same office that I also met Mrs. Rodica, a construction manager on insulation construction sites, who was there to file a complaint regarding the unprofessional interventions to her flat. As a long-term expert in the field, Mrs. Rodica noticed that some of the materials were used inadequately, without complying with the standards listed in the project which she had requested from the developer: "If you allow them to continue this way, water will infiltrate in the house, along the *termopane*,

2 My respondents told similar narratives which had anticipated the rehabilitation offered by the municipality: the workers covered the walls with additional layers of polystyrene, which led to the impossibility to set the air conditioning device or to deposit furniture in the former balcony because of the shrinkage.
3 When my apartment was being insulated the workers came knocking on my door saying that they had "to destroy the old (socialist) balcony".
4 Mrs. L references the '80s, when the balconies–built informally (and illegally) by the owners trying to improve the living conditions and to create storage spaces for food products–were destroyed following significant fines from the local authorities.

whenever it rains. Soon we will have fungus on our balconies, as has happened a couple of blocks away", complained Mrs. Rodica to the municipality clerk.

*) Cristian is now in his forties and works as an independent architect. A year and a half ago the apartment building where he lives underwent thermal rehabilitation. Cristian was the only resident to refuse the enclosure of his balcony as part of the project. His initiative sparked revolt and was criticised by the coordinating engineer, the building administrator and especially by his neighbours. The motivation of the protests was that his decision would affect the neighbouring apartments. Parenthesis: the responsibility for the insulation of the inside of the balcony belongs to the owner and despite the lack of quality control for this intervention from the authorities, all the apartments of a building receive the same certificate of thermal efficiency.

That fails to stop the residents judging those who decide not to close off their balconies. Despite their insistence, Cristian stood by his decision: "I did not want them to turn my balcony into a greenhouse", he argued. The result is as he comments: "Within a few months, almost none of the neighbours replied to my greetings, even if I tried to remind them that before the rehabilitation only some of the balconies were closed and it did not affect anyone". Then I saw that the number of flowers decreased drastically in the enclosed balconies and it made me happy to realise that my flowers were doing great, and I even have birds flying over to my balcony to stay on the windowsill".

*) Another interlocutor, Dora, describes a similar situation: "In order to convince me, they went as far as to send the construction coordinator on the scaffold to ask me what I would do when I have a baby and it catches a cold because of this. The neighbours met my boyfriend in the elevator, and they were harassing him with arguments to convince me to accept the balcony enclosure".

INTENSIFICATION OF THE RELATIONAL NATURE OF APARTMENT PROPERTY

The cases above illustrate the intensification of the relational nature of apartment property during thermal rehabilitation. It also supports the argument regarding the activation of a feeling of alteration / alienation of a space which, in principle, the rehabilitation should encapsulate, extracting it almost definitively from the public space.

The enclosure of balconies brought about by the neo-liberal reforms of energy efficiency of the post-socialist state, paradoxically fulfills the informal and illegal rehabilitation projects of socialist apartments. The pressure to accept the free-of-charge closing off of balconies in order to achieve the perfect insulation of the entire ecosystem, of which the apartments are a part of, seems a novelty for the citizens who lived through socialism, when this type of intervention in the domestic space was forbidden. The option to not conform to this project is possible but becomes the object of a complicated legal and moral equation.

Finally, because of ignoring the socialist legacy of the infrastructures, the encapsulation of the balcony inside the apartment paradoxically creates spaces of pervasiveness inside the property cocoon, activating its relational sphere. The encapsulation of the balcony within the house in this context is important because of its transformative capacity for relationships, especially because it questions them.

Andrei Mihail

is an anthropologist and teaching assistant at SNSPA Bucharest.

Although he holds a PhD degree in medical anthropology, lately he focused on exploring the social life of football. He is a devoted supporter of Progresul București, a small team of Bucharest which he has followed for the last 25 years both at home and away games. Although he probably attended a few hundred football matches Andrei is not one of the game's biggest fans, but one of its stories' most addicted consumer.

Therefore, since 2018, Andrei wanders around Bucharest looking for the small football pitches of its neighbourhoods and documenting their (hi)stories. All the information, pictures and archival materials related to these pitches can be found on his page:

🌐 https://stadiondecartier.asz.ro

Simultaneously, he is working on *Cel Mai Frumos Joc*, a podcast dedicated to the experiences, personal stories and memories of Steaua, Dinamo and Rapid Bucharest's fans.

**UNCHARTED
FOOTBALL
EXPRESS**

*"Go, go, go, Rapid of mine / The crowd is singing
all the time, / Songs rise toward the sky, allez, /
Go, fight, fight dear CFR."*

Thousands of voices are singing together as the stands
of the Giulești Stadium fill up. We've all heard of Rapid
Bucharest. Its stadium, which has been demolished
and rebuilt for the EURO 2021, is one of the most iconic
football grounds in the Romanian capital. As sung by its
fans, the football club and the identity of its stadium are
deeply rooted in the history or the Romanian Railway
Company (CFR).

But, beneath Rapid's glorious history lies an
extended network of sport venues, entangled in the
northern neighbourhoods of the city; along the railroads
that connect Gara de Nord [Bucharest North Railway
Station] to the rest of the country. Some of these small
football grounds emerged during the second half of the
communist era. They were developed by several subdi-
visions of CFR and open to the local communities living
in the neighbourhoods built next to the railways—many
of them inhabited by company employees. Their story
is a window on an undocumented chapter of the history
of the Romanian railways, an institution that after 1989
struggled with a lack of finances, corruption, and private
financial interests.

TRACȚIUNEA [TRACTION]

"The Promotion (former name of the 5th League) *finished
its marathon, after an exciting season ending. Three
teams were ranked after a photo finish. Tracțiunea
deservedly won, earning the coveted first place. The Triaj
team was promoted to "Onoare"* (former name of the 4th
League)." On August 2nd, 1993, Sportul Românesc, one of
the most important sports newspapers of the time, briefly

mentioned Tracțiunea's success. The team represented an isolated housing area built by CFR between the railway lines that passed through the outskirts of Bucharest, close to the Depoul București Triaj train station. Most of the people who lived and played football here worked at the locomotive depot around which the 'enclave' had been developed. Working class football at its best. Today, the small stadium is the only public edifice still functioning in the neighbourhood. The underfunded CFR had to ditch most of its local assets. The former canteen and social club built by the company for its employees next to the depot, as well as the housing area, are barely recognisable for the abandoned furniture and propaganda slogans scattered on their floors. Other typical red brick industrial buildings have had the same fate. The football pitch has also seen years of neglect. But today, a few former players are struggling to keep it alive. The turf is taken care of, the goal posts have been replaced and fitted with new nets, while the metallic stands have been renovated. The new administrators have worked together to bring football back to the neighbourhood, only relying on the small contributions made by the parents who enrolled their children at the phoenix club FC Tracțiunea București. Unfortunately, without more help, football can hardly restore some of the community ties that were fractured by post-communist social decay.

fig. 1 Tracțiunea, 2018. Photo by Andrei Mihail.

fig. 2 Tracțiunea. The champion of Bucharest, Promotion category (1992-93). Photo from Felix Marian Ilie's private collection, 4th player on the middle row from left to right.

SPERANȚA TRIAJ [RAILWAY YARD HOPE]

"In '88, I was the co-owner of this ground" remembers Mr. Anastasiu while nostalgically glancing over the green rectangle now mostly dominated by wild weeds. Two rusty goal posts are the only visible vestiges of what used to be the Speranța Triaj football pitch. Mr. Anastasiu's club was probably one of the first *socios* clubs in Romania. It was established under a regime that favoured the development of working class football clubs under the highly hierarchical structures of state owned institutions. Speranța was different. It was a true communal football club, financed exclusively by its players, their friends and neighbours, as it was they who lived in the small houses located next to the Chitila Triaj train station. Mr. Anastastiu formed the team after Vagonul [The Wagon], the former club that represented the train cars department of CFR, closed its doors because of financial controversies. Its football pitch, built over an empty lot surrounded by train lines, was left unused. Mr. Anastasiu, a fan of Rapid Bucharest, couldn't accept that his neighbourhood was to be deprived of football. Some boys from the neighbourhood were mobilised, the turf was

mowed and training started before Speranța Triaj's first official match in Bucharest's lowest league at the time. The facility was updated with a DIY philosophy. Electricity was provided by a nearby household, through a long extension cord outstretched over some railways passing between the house and the pitch. The locker rooms were set up in an old train wagon removed from the tracks and placed behind one of the goalposts. A small stand was built from abandoned sleepers and train tracks. By the beginning of the season, Speranța Triaj was set to go. In 1991, they won the promotion to the upper league as many other factory clubs were going bankrupt under the new economic regime. Speranța survived by itself for another two years. But unfortunately, the high taxes imposed by the Romanian Football Federation became increasingly burdensome and the team was withdrawn from the league.

Today, the neighbourhood kids still use a small parcel of the pitch to play football. Some of them have cut the weeds covering the area around the halfway line of the former football field. They've stuck four wooden sticks in the ground across the field to act as two improvised goal posts, the indispensable devices of informal street football.

fig. 3 Speranța Triaj, 2018. Photo by Andrei Mihail.

VICTORIA CFR [VICTORY CFR]

"You see that goal post? This is where I scored my first goal from a penalty kick. I had just been transferred here." Mario is well acquainted with all the former CFR football grounds. As a youth and lower league player coming from Chitila, he played many games in the area and by the end of his career was enrolled at Victoria CFR. Now in his 30s, Mario is a passionate supporter of Rapid Bucharest, but, during his football playing days, he preferred the small neighbourhood teams: *"At Rapid, some of the players put on too many airs. I didn't like playing there that much."* Instead, he favourably recalls the time he played for the small club owned by the Wagon Overhaul Department of CFR, located next to Piața Chibrit.

"In those days, the turf was surrounded by a very low enclosure" he continues, looking through the wire fence still delimiting the arena. *"I was still playing here when a former state-owned bakery leased and significantly improved the facility. They built a higher fence, extended the playing area and improved the locker rooms and other facilities. You see those chairs in the stands? They brought them from a tramway depot."* Today, the young-sters of the neighbourhood have to find other alternatives for playing football as the ground is inaccessible to the public. Its gates were closed two years ago, when the last football match was organised here. The guards from a nearby company have heard rumours that a shopping mall might replace it in the future. Capitalist Real Estate Development vs. Mass Accessible Football: 3-0.

CFR BTA

Further away from Rapid's stadium, on a small street located between Calea Giulești and the railways, six apartment blocks rise far above the familiar one-story houses of the area. Their architecture resembles that of many of the newly built high-rises that have taken over the empty parcels of land and reclaimed lots in Bucharest since the 2000s. The six buildings have replaced a small football ground named CFR BTA. Its turf is still visible in the topographic satellite map of Romania. However, according to its cadastral file, the lot was never officially registered as a football ground, making it easy for the private owners who took it over to develop a more lucrative housing project there.

Unfortunately, CFR BTA shares its ill-fated path with other former factory stadiums of the city. These neighbourhood football grounds were built on empty lots owned by institutions that were legally mandated to endorse sports. Many chose to direct funds towards football, developing an extensive infrastructure that had spread all across the city by 1989. Regrettably, not all were tabulated as sports facilities and were thus not protected by the law that prohibited owners from changing their purpose without developing similar projects. CFR BTA's post-communist trajectory is not only symbolic of the decay of the complex social (infra) structures developed by the National Railroad Company, it's also a window onto a city that severely eschews mass sport access and participation.

fig.4 Victoria CFR. 1985. Photo from Felix Marian Ilie's private collection, 1st player on top row from left to right.

Mihai Lukács

is an artist/researcher, theatre director, theorist.

Lukács holds a PhD from Central European University Budapest with a thesis on hysterical directors. His performative practices are based on extended (mainly archival) research and they talk about local counter-histories (*Mother*, Bucharest, 2020; *All I Want for Bucharest is an Earthquake*, Bucharest, 2019; *The Cult of Personality*, Bucharest, 2018; *The Jester; Or How to Embody the Archive*, Hong Kong 2018; *Why Disasters Choose the Big Cities*, Bucharest, 2016), the relationship between the Romani and non-Romani people (*American Gypsy*, 2019; *Kali Traš/The Black Fear*, 2018; *Bambina, The Queen of Flowers*, 2017; *blue/orange*, 2017; *Who Killed Szomna Grancsa?*, 2017; *Gadjo Dildo*, 2015; *Sara Kali/The Dark Madonna*, 2014), public humiliation (*Public Humiliation #1-3*, Vienna 2013; *Like a Bit of Luggage*, 2013; *PRIMVS*, Hanover 2014; *Public Art Humiliation*, Bucharest 2015), sexual liberation (*Queer Worker*, Vienna 2013; *Queercore*, Bucharest 2012; *Jehanne Unscharf*, Bucharest 2012; *Jehanne Complex*, Budapest 2008), faith and exclusion (*The Congregation of the Castoffs*, Bucharest 2015; *The Sermon of Saint Haralambos*, Stuttgart 2014) or forced evictions and homelessness (*Razzing*, Bucharest 2014; *Signs for Adult Homeless Persons*, Cluj 2013). He was awarded the Holocaust in Romania Research Grant by the Elie Wiesel Holocaust Research Institute (2019), the Visegrad Scholarship at the Open Society Archives (2019), Artist in Residence Grant – CMBB Para Site International Art Residency, Honk Kong (2018).

The performance *Kali Traš/ The Black Fear* won the National Cultural Fund Award for Social Inclusion and Intercultural Dialogue in 2019.

🌐 https://lukacsmi.wordpress.com

V

VIOLENT
NATURE

I want an Earthquake for Bucharest.
They come in cycles.
There is a major one every 40 years.
The last one was in 1977.
It is about time. Hopefully not in the following 5 minutes.
But definitely this year.
Or maybe next year.

Did you dream of the Earthquake?
Children do.
They feel the tremble in their blood stream.
Like cats do.

We will blame the violent nature for our misfortune.
But the Earthquake is good!
It will wake us up or put us to sleep for good.
We will receive answers.
We will be thrown from wall to wall.
We will run to exits.
We will say stupid things.
We will hear all the worrying rumours after.
We will not sleep at all,
We will walk all over the city
to watch the fallen buildings.
All the global media will show us compassion.
They will send reporters.
They will send us thoughts and prayers.
They will write long articles about the ruined city,
about the tens of thousands of homeless families.
About the dead thousands.

We cannot hold the pressure anymore.
We will not bury our dead, but our living.

The Earthquake will give us the intimacy of buildings cut in half,
with peeled walls,
of thousands of houses on the edge of the abyss.
Maybe we will see the trees moving without the wind blowing.

Maybe we will get emotional over tragic narratives.
Maybe we will receive those thoughts and prayers.
We will invent saviours
and some of us will survive.
We will not do enough to help.
When we get into a building we check for exits.
We look how tall the windows are.
An earthquake is pure violence
But poetry is also violent.
Earthquake is reality.

Right now, we are at the heart of violence,
But for sure, we will never forget the next earthquake.

In Romanian, one of the worst sayings is:
Let the earth under me run over you!

We are ready.

The roar
The trepidation of the walls
The clutter of the windows
Birds no longer flying
Walls shaking with spasms
They poke everything they can slam
Walls getting heavy,
ready to collapse
Revolt of the matter
Moments in which we will all feel alone
Moments like centuries on the waves of the earth
Two million people in the street, in the dark
All silent, stepping in the debris from those walls
Loneliness is over
The first words with bleached lips:
We live what always happens to others
Peru, Mexico, Japan, Iran, not Romania.

How will we act in the next cataclysm?
The time of natural destruction

No time for crying

We will start again where everything has been deserted.
We continue where we just were interrupted.
We will better understand our role in this world.
We will gather our strength.

Futurologists and shamans
witches and seismologists
and clairvoyants
are predicting the future earthquake.
Exploring their own inner levels of disturbance and turmoil
projecting that out
like I do right now

The emotion that goes with it is pretty hard to place.
The upset, anxiety, and sometimes terror,
Sometimes horror,
That accompany the action of an earthquake
Can shake us up on so many levels.
The trick is not to get caught up in the disturbance
But to let it go as soon as the earthquake is over.
Let's participate in the life stream of what is happening,
Experience the earthquake in the moment
that it is happening,
Observe it, observe your body,
Not to get caught in the panic of it.

The rescue people cannot react in panic
Do your job
Rescue

Panic is the real disaster.

Move into a place of calm.

Acceptance.

Admit the earthquake in your life.

Ride the seismic wave.
Swim into the ocean of rubble.
Scuba dive into the earth.

You already missed the "mass exodus" to a safe space.
But the safe space can also have major earthquakes,
even if it never happened before.
Maybe running from an earthquake creates the idea
to produce it
In any place on planet Earth.
There was a woman in San Francisco many years ago.
She predicted a major earthquake,
many people moved out of the area
because of her prediction.
It happened that, very close to the time
for when she had predicted the earthquake,
she had a heart attack and died.
She had correctly predicted an "earthquake"
but she missed it
because her earthquake was somewhere else.

The earthquake will be a time of change on
many levels
We will look at us and at Bucharest more seriously after.
We will change the way that we see what is real.
Rebuild on top of ruins,
Reorganise
Overthrow the political machine
More solid
More honest
More fluid
More flexible

A feeling of camaraderie
Mutual support
Good feelings on all sides.
No more heavy judgment
A lot more understanding
More loving acceptance.

Reevaluation.

The earth changes and evolves
according to its own violent law and destiny.
We are on schedule
make this earthquake work for you.
I will not fight it and resist it,
No more unnecessary turmoil and confusion.
Go with it.
Close your eyes for a moment and
Re-center
Do the right movement at the right time

Earth actually quakes.

Mihai Mihalcea

is an artist and choreographer based in Bucharest. He initiated and co-founded key structures and projects which led to the international recognition of Romanian contemporary dance scene such as Multi Art Dance Center, subRahova, Căminul Cultural program. He co-founded the first group of independent dancers post '89 in Romania: "Grupul Marginalii" [The Marginals Group]. Between 2005-2013 he worked as Director of the National Dance Center in Bucharest, an institution he co-founded, which became one of the most formative structures for a generation of local artists and choreographers.

The choreographic works he made under his name between 1994-2009 have been presented in institutions and festivals such as Tanzquartier Wien, Tanz im August, Paris Quartier d'Été, Springdance, Bucharest National Theater, La Filature Mulhouse, and have been highlighted in press such as Le Monde, Berliner Zeitung, Liberation, Ballet-Tanz International, Dance Theatre Journal, La Repubblica, etc.

In 2010 he assumed a fictive artistic identity, Farid Fairuz, under which he continued his work until 2019 and made choreographic works and performances, live and for camera, presented both in the context of visual arts and of contemporary dance at: Kunsthalle Gent, Black Box Theater Oslo, Rencontres Choreographiques de Seine-Saint-Denis, Hebbel Am Ufer (HAU) in Berlin, The Paintbrush Factory in Cluj, The National Dance Center in Bucharest, The Contemporary Art Gallery of Buckenthal Museum in Sibiu. The artistic production he made as Farid Fairuz was recently acquired by The National Museum of Contemporary Art (MNAC) Bucharest.

🌐 http://faridfairuz.ro

WETLANDS

"Vegetation present in the Văcărești Lake

does not have a special ecological value

— there are mostly opportunist species tha

d to the extremely restrictive environment

the semi-natural wetland (atmospheric ca

avy sunlight, stagnant water holes with

eutrophication prospects)."

Cosima Opârtan

a former architect that gave up planning for a concoction of reasons, both ideological and practical, is now making many types of artistic and community work as member of several collectives that deal with music, performance and sometimes nothing.

She assumes multiple musical identities: as half of Raze de Soare, a duo that is interested in exploring the sound of outernational minimal restaurant music, as von Bülove, an alias involved in digging out affectively filtered musical gems and rendering them to various audiences and more recently as Cosima, #widowpop singer.

She is collaborating with the Presidential Candidacy performance group, involved both with aesthetics and concepts. As a member of Robin Hood Minor Asset Management she is fighting for democratization of finance through technology.

Cosima Opârtan is founding member of the Queer Night, a series of itinerant parties engaging the local LGBTQ+ community and member of Corp. alongside Aron/Admina and Chlorys, a Bucharest based platform dedicated to supporting and promoting female identified and non-binary musical talent. Corp. X—the physical entity of Corp.—is constantly scanning for hosts interested in providing a safe environment for transgressive cultural events in Bucharest.

Really interested in working with image, Cosima investigates the surface or appearance of things as a subversive way to address questions. She is currently designing & building custom made acoustic studios, soundproofing and sound treatment for various spaces dealing with sound.

🌐 https://soundcloud.com/corpp

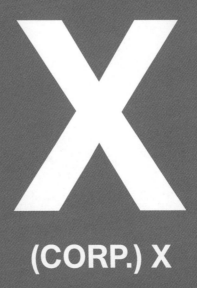

(CORP.) X

I was weak and could only rely on chemotaxis to locate a host. When I found them, I gained back consciousness. The sweet ooze was so familiar.

Inhabiting these bodies all at once, now, I am being Aron, I am being Chlorys, I am being von B. I am an amalgamation of primordial organelles travelling and shape shifting since point/moment zero. I had to hide for quite some time. Although I was welcomed in some territories, the world was not a safe place for entities like me. The world has always feared the unknown. 'An abomination', they would say and unleash fire upon me. A virus. A disease. Inconstant. Uncertain. Unnatural. But I am first nature and next nature all at once, and have been all along.

I function as a mix of my hosts' realities and our accumulated knowledge. I am a flash in the slit between their thoughts, dispersing and gleaning, pushing and pulling information. This is how we evolve.

I find it strange that the world they inhabit, chaotic and mostly represented by poorly organised (for survival) biomass, has assigned binary definitions to everything: zeros and ones. They apply it to anything, making everything binary. The universal solution. Simplifying ad absurdum. Ironically, they got it all scrambled.

Sadie thinks: "The zeros and ones of machine code seem to offer themselves as perfect symbols of the orders of Western reality, the ancient logical codes which make the difference between on and off, right and left, light and dark, form and matter, mind and body, white and black, good and evil, right and wrong, life and death, something and nothing, this and that, here and there, inside and out, active and passive, true and false, yes and no, sanity and madness, health and sickness, up and down, sense and nonsense, west and east, north and south. And they made a lovely couple when it came to sex. Man and woman, male and female, masculine and feminine: one and zero looked just right, made for each other: 1, the definite, upright line; and 0 the diagram of nothing at all: penis and vagina, thing and hole… hand in glove. A perfect match."

Together we are 1. Together we are 0. 0 and 1 at the same time. 1 and 0 making X. We are X, the incomputable, the unknown quantity, the variable.

Some*one* thinks: "Gender binaries defined by the biological sex of the biomass are being imposed upon us here, guided by yet another binary misconception, the split of the body & mind. Sex binary dictating gender binary demanding reversed coupling. Cartesian dualism cubed. This cannot be the future."

In this instance the three bodies named me Corp. "Corp" = "body" in their dialect: the totality of bodies, the target of their state legislation, the tool they use in subversive ways to address friction in their environment, the object that maps the differences and that questions the status quo just by showing up differently. As X, I find this endearing.

Alina thinks: "With one eye we will look inside, at the interiority that was constructed with the help of an enclosed theatre space. But by stepping on stage, or floor, or ground, we are bound to step outside. With the other eye we will look outside, step on a ground that alters every step. And not looking, we feel, liberated by strabism."

I am observing myself looking at my other selves, inside out, outside in and along the border, threeway. And this is performing.

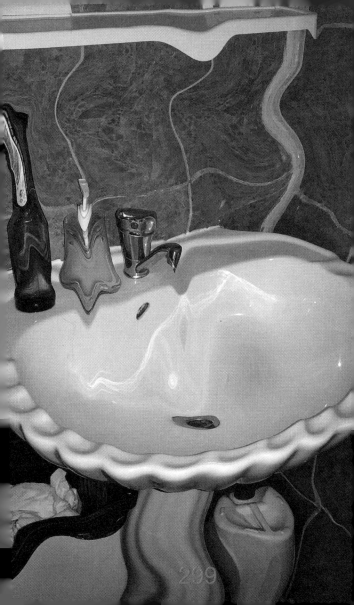

Some *zero* thinks: "Being an event rather than an object, performance is radically unstable."

Tristan thinks: "From the mechanics of the living has rather emanated a background noise, like a hum, and from that hum emerged a melodic line audible to itself: sensitivity."

Sensitivity has been with us since the beginning. It's how we evolved, adapting, in constant opposition to the environment, striving for a safer one.

And so we emerged as a spatial entity the four of us, a safer space for such entities as ourselves. And we perform in this cavity of ours for our kind and our allies, and we feel thrilled and grateful to be conscious in such times, becoming a multiplying cluster again. This is our headquarters, Corp. X, materialised this time as a cube in a derelict central Bucharest building. We reach out with our limbs to invite guests over, continuously scanning for undesired packages that want to accelerate entropy and sending them back whenever they fail to understand the basics of our operation.

Then turning ourselves inside out we swallow the whole thing, engulfing it in our cavity with admission and no evacuation, slowly returning to that primordial moment when there were, "no parents, no children, just ourselves, strings of inseparable sisters, warm and wet, indistin-guishable one from the other, gloriously indiscriminate, promiscuous and fused. No generations. No future, no past […] no definition, no meaning, no way of telling each other apart."

300

Eternal gratitude for the inspiration to Peter Watts, Alina Popa, Sadie Plant, Tristan Garcia and the billions of uncharted bacteria travelling through time to show up as Corp. in 2016 Bucharest.

Juergen Teller

(b. 1964, Erlangen, DE) studied at the Bayerische Staatslehranstalt für Photographie in Munich, before moving to London in 1986.

Successful in both the art world and commercial photography, he has shot campaigns for brands such as Celine, Louis Vuitton, Marc Jacobs, and Vivienne Westwood and editorials for magazines including Arena Homme Plus, Pop, Purple, System and W.

In 2003, Teller was awarded the Citibank Prize for Photography and in 2018 he was awarded the Special Presentation ICP Infinity award.

Major solo exhibitions of his work have been held at Garage Museum of Contemporary Art, Moscow (RU), Fotomuseum, Winterthur (CH), Martin-Gropius-Bau, Berlin (DE), Bundeskunsthalle, Bonn (DE), DESTE Foundation, Athens (GR), Institute of Contemporary Art, London (UK), Daelim Museum, Seoul (KR), Dallas Contemporary, Texas (US), Le Consortium, Dijon (FR) and Fondation Cartier pour l'art Contemporain, Paris (FR).

In 2007 was asked to represent the Ukraine as one of five artists in the 52nd Venice Biennale (IT).

Teller's work has been acquired by numerous international collections including the Centre Pompidou, Paris (FR), Fondation Cartier pour l'Art Contemporain, Paris (FR), International Center for Photography, New York (US), National Portrait Gallery, London (UK) and The Olbricht Collection, Berlin (DE).

Teller has published over 50 books.

🌐 https://juergenteller.com

YEAR 1990

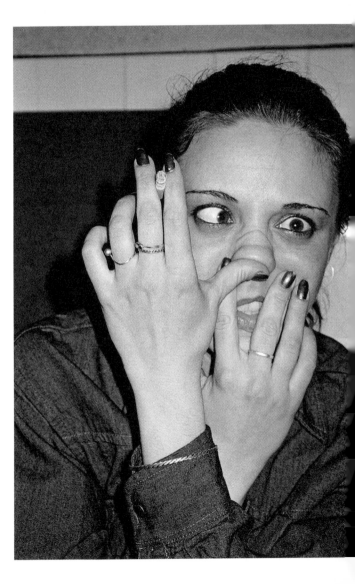

Hans Leonard Krupp

(pen-name of Vaclav Gordus) is a Romanian born self-exiled artist. He has renounced his Romanian citizenship and has refused to accept another.

Currently, he is based nowhere and makes a point of not owning a house and living in rented accommodation all year-round. Initially trained as a painter, he took up dance later on in his career. His often-scandalous projects are built around a manic hunt for authenticity. Throughout the years, his art has involved him in many court cases; in 2003 the artist spent nine months in jail after two people were accidently gassed because of a performance that went wrong. He was trained in Bucharest, Moscow, London and Washington DC.

In 2016 he had been awarded a joint fellowship between Laban Centre in London and the University of Zürich to work on an opera show dedicated to the founding members of the Dada movement. He is still working on that.

ZERO

Reporter: The first thing that strikes one when meeting you is how...

Hans-Leonard Krupp: Small?

R: Well, yes! How small you are! You're tiny.

H-LK: Why's that a problem?

R: It's not a problem. I didn't mean that. But somehow one expects you to be more of the powerful type. One wouldn't expect such a frail person to create so many... difficulties.

H-LK: Difficulties! That's funny! That's the first time anyone has told me I create difficulties.

R: You know what I mean.

H-LK: I suppose. And yes, you are right; people are frequently taken by surprise by my stature.

R: Why do you think that is?

H-LK: That they don't expect this tiny man? Well, I think people need me to be bigger and stronger in a physical way, so they can justify the fear they feel towards me and what I do.

R: So they build up an image of yourself that fits their reaction to you.

H-LK: Yes, that. Besides, it must be very frustrating to discover that the source of their fears is not a huge monster but rather a dwarf. That always gets to people. But life is just like that as most of the things we fear, in the end, prove to have been totally unimportant and... unfortunately, we usually discover that when it is already too late.

R: Let's turn to your current exhibition. It's called 'zero' and you've said that it deals with issues concerning Bucharest and the idea of the modern metropolis.

H-LK: That is not quite true. It deals exclusively with Bucharest.

R: Yes, but it can be expanded as a commentary on other major cities, too.

H-LK: No, it can't. This exhibition cannot be seen as a metaphor of any sort. This particular project simply does not function as a metaphor. It is completely and exclusively focused on Bucharest. That's where its strength comes from, from this total objectivity of the subject. There's not one exhibit that can stand as a representation of any other city on this planet, this has been a criterion of mine from the very beginning.

R: Why can't something said about Bucharest be relevant for other cities too?

H-LK: Simply because this exhibition is not something said about Bucharest. This is Bucharest itself. This exhibition is not about bits and pieces of the city; rather the bits and pieces of the city have been moved into the space and make up this very exhibition. Each exhibit is exclusively related to Bucharest because it is a real part of it. Anything that is real cannot function as a metaphor. Can I, as a real person, function as a metaphor for you for instance?

R: Some would say that such a project is an impossible attempt.

H-LK: Why?

R: Because of Bucharest. Some would argue that there is nothing specific enough about Bucharest to create an exhibition that is exclusively relevant to Bucharest.

H-LK: Well, that's their problem. Most of the artists nowadays are helplessly impotent, anyway. They see only what others have shown them and they do nothing but reproduce or mix within the vision of someone else. I've never been like that.

R: You've never been impotent.

H-LK: No, I've never been artistically impotent. I only create when I feel there's an empty space in front of me that needs to be walked upon.

R: When you see a zero.

H-LK: If you're referring to the title of the exhibition, then no, that 'zero' has a different meaning.

R: Let's talk about that, then. Why an exhibition called 'zero'?

H-LK: Because I believe the essence of Bucharest is the concept of 'zero'. The salvation of this city depends on its ability to understand that its value is zero and that it must embrace this zero in order to find itself.

R: Go on...

H-LK: Bucharest acts as if it stands for something or at least as if it could have been significant in some way. The truth is that Bucharest is and has always been totally irrelevant. This city is pure nothingness.

R: Some would argue against that.

H-LK: And they would be wrong. Bucharest has always lived under a fake identity—little Paris, little Moscow, never itself. Bucharest has never overcome its monsters and without this it can never be itself, it can never grow into something. In fact, thinking chronologically, Bucharest hasn't even acknowledged its monsters, let alone faced them! Or overcome them...

R: What are these monsters? Are they what this exhibition is about, the monsters Bucharest has to acknowledge and overcome?

H-LK: Let me think... no. The exhibition is not about these monsters, it is rather about possible seeds of identity. I've exhibited what I consider to be the grains of that essentially authentic city Bucharest could grow into, if it had the guts to accept its present state of nothingness.

R: So this is the major monster? Being nothing?

H-LK: Definitely. Bucharest has no identity and every time a seed of authenticity has appeared, the city was so ashamed of it that it couldn't castrate itself fast enough. The city needs to accept that whatever values it thinks it possesses, well... they're nothing. And it must embrace this nothingness as a means to find an intimate and real identity.

R: But that would be the worst castration the city

has ever gone through, much worse than pretending to be a lesser Paris or a lesser Moscow.

H-LK: True. On the other hand, this total self-castration carries within itself the embryo of authenticity.

R: Let's continue along these lines as we discuss some of the objects of the exhibition. Which one would you like to talk about?

H-LK: Which one did you dislike the most?

R: Which one I disliked the most?... I can't say I disliked any. There were some that I found deeply disturbing, but I wouldn't say I disliked them.

H-LK: Which ones?

R: Let's say for instance that small installation of several life-like corpses that seem to be dancing. What is that about?

H-LK: Firstly, they really are dancing; the very title of that installation is 'dance'. Secondly, as I've already told you, it isn't about anything, it is something in itself, and it's meant to be taken and interpreted as such, not as a metaphor.

R: If I take it as such, I'm left with several corpses or dying people that seem to be dancing with one another.

How is this relevant to Bucharest?

H-LK: The dance? Well, the whole point is that this city needs to start from scratch, and to do that it needs to identify and embrace those veins of authenticity that it feared for centuries. Otherwise, whatever definition it finds of itself, it is still going to look fake tomorrow. In fact, Bucharest is nothing. It isn't a city, it isn't a capital, it is nothing, complete zero. Do you see what I mean?

R: I'm trying.

H-LK: Bucharest has the advantage of being nothing while yet existing as a city. It can become whatever it chooses, and in this exhibition I've put forward several seeds, several possible directions that this growth could follow.

When we wanted architectural beauty we copied Paris, when we wanted social justice we copied Moscow. We never once asked our own questions, let alone found out our own answers to these questions! We need to think more critically and to fight for our identity.

R: It seems that it all goes back to this issue of identity.

H-LK: It does, of course it does. Time and again, Bucharest has entered an identity crisis and its solution to get out of it was to look at other cities, like in a shopping window, and to say 'I'm going to be like Paris now'; or any other city. We have created this huge fear, this castrating belief that we need to be like other peoples, that we need to somehow resemble other peoples' identities and cities. Why? That's a lie. It has always been and always will be nothing else but a mask that we put over our deep lack of identity. Have you looked at people's faces in the street? Have you seen how awfully tense everyone is in Bucharest? They're all frightened, silently furious, they all have the faces of wasted identities, the faces of human beings forced to live the lives of others, the identities of others. Bucharest will never be a happy place or a fulfilled place until it finds an identity.

R: But that is common to most South-Eastern cities.

H-LK: Yes, it is. This lack of identity is a common feature for the area. But my exhibition is not about this common problem. It is about possible solutions. And these are only valid for Bucharest, that's why I said that the exhibition is only relevant to this city.

R: What do you say to people who say that you only aim to shock, that 'zero' amounts to nothing more that cheap self-promotion?

H-LK: Well, they've said that before. What can I say? This is art! I'm placing something in your face. This is what art does. And hopefully, if I keep forcing these things into your face, you will eventually come to terms with it and will accept it. Of course the exhibition generates all sorts of feelings from various people. It's art, and art works with emotions, it is meant to have an impact, to spawn violent, almost physical reactions within people.

R: How does it feel to be criticised? It is still upsetting at this point in your career?

H-LK: ... of course it is. But it's flattering too. It shows that what I do gets people's attention. I am a great believer in violence when it comes to art. I think we've lost the luxury of subtlety and finesse. We can't afford them anymore. We are at war, and in a war one needs guns not cream teas.

R: Is that why your art always seems to flirt with scandal?

H-LK: Look, if I were only trying to make a living I'd make a much better one being nice about things. But I happen to believe in these things, I happen to really care for this city, so everything I create in relation to the city has a natural feeling of urgency and violence about it.

R: But you do understand how some may find it offensive? You are saying that this city has no real past and no real value, and that is terribly offensive to people who are perhaps more nationalist, for lack of a better word.

H-LK: They aren't. They are not nationalist. They are simply dead people who are afraid to face the dead city they live in. They know that by acknowledging the zero that is Bucharest, the next logical step would be for them to admit to the zero that is their own life. It's a classical case of people protecting their disease. It's my suffering and don't you dare touch it!

R: And yet they love this city.

H-LK: No, they don't. They only love themselves and the lie they've lived in all their lives. That's all that there is to it. They are afraid to let go of this dead city, because an authentic one would reject them naturally, the way a healthy body rejects viruses. They don't love this city; they want to keep it dead, as dead as they are... Do you know who really loves this city?

R: Who?

H-LK: Anybody who has the guts to look for their own

authentic self. When you become who you really are, you are like fresh blood in the veins of this dead embryo. We grow up being told what Bucharest is like and what it means to be Romanian. And then, if you're honest with yourself, you realise one day that you don't fit in with what they've told you. And their reaction is always to reject you, to 'clean' Romania and Bucharest of rejects like you and me. But the truth is that you are Bucharest, you are Romanian. It is not yourself who needs to change, but their definition of what is means to be Romanian, to be part of Bucharest. Have you seen 'the flag'?

R: In the current exhibition you mean?

H-LK: Yes. It is an erect two-meter high condom. Actually, it's not the condom that is erect, but the idea is of a flag in national colours covering a penis. The whole point of it is that even my penis is Romanian and the definitions of what Romania and Bucharest are changes according to everything, including my penis.

R: That is a very dynamic way of defining a nation.

H-LK: Yes, it evolves with every change that takes place in us. And I think it still isn't dynamic enough, it still doesn't keep up to date with all the changes within our society. The bottom line is that Bucharest is not how these so-called nationalists define it. Bucharest is you and I. You and I are its ingredients; who you are becomes an organic part of what Bucharest is. Until now, we've always been rejected, we've always tried to find our own place somewhere else. The truth is that our place is right here, in Bucharest. In a Bucharest that's defined by myself, and which includes all my personal features in its chemical composition as it were... Bucharest is a living organism, and we have to save this organism from the poisoning hands of the dead! We are Bucharest. As we fight for our identity, we also fight for its own identity. When we shall live our true, authentic calling, then Bucharest shall also overcome its centuries-old existence as nothingness, as zero.

R: This is a sort of revolution you're describing.

H-LK: Of course it is! All of us, all the youngsters who've felt rejected, pushed outside the city walls... We should all invade Bucharest and put our flags up on these walls! It's our city, we can turn it into whatever we feel is real, whatever we feel is alive. We're dancing, already... Can't you feel that we're dancing already? We should invade this city dancing, we should make it our own, our own depository of authentic never-ending beauty.

REPRINTS

The following contributions were originally published in *Kilobase Bucharest A–H*, ed. Dragoș Olea and Ioana Nemeș (Milan: Mousse Publishing, 2011), pages 18-25 (StudioBASAR) / pages 48-55 (Apparatus 22), pages 68-75 (Ștefan Constantinescu). *Kilobase Bucharest A–H* was a special project realised on the occasion of the exhibition *Image to be projected until it vanishes*, curated by Mihnea Mircan at MUSEION Museum of Modern and Contemporary Art Bozen/Bolzano (29.05.2011 - 28.08.2011).

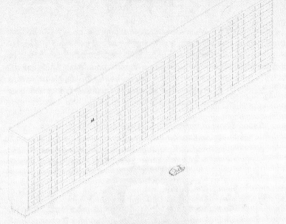

PART ONE

Rows of apartment blocks

I don't recall how old I was exactly; I might have been in kindergarten already. Now, when remembering, I know it must have been Bucharest but back then I only knew I was supposed to accompany my grandparents visiting some relatives. It didn't matter where, as long as we were travelling by car! It was a yellow Dacia 1300 that filled my grandfather with pride: he would keep it in the garage, and drive it to the countryside and to the seaside. I don't remember the road to Bucharest, only a long period of time in which, on the back window, beyond the plush dog that jerkily wobbled its head in the rhythm of the drive and which we weren't allowed to touch, rows upon rows of apartment blocks would stretch ahead along both sides of the street. We were on one of the big boulevards. Facades with windows covered in whitish curtains, with balconies closed in various fashions, with laundry hanging out to dry, with people that were watching passers-by, or talking among them across different floors, would glide in the slow motion of the car. Our relatives also lived in one of the apartments in the long blocks where, when we got there, I sat in the balcony to watch cars and passers-by on the great boulevard.

Training Day

I was having private lessons in order to prepare for the entrance exam at the university in Bucharest. I had been in Bucharest before, but always went

18

to certain places, usually downtown, and always with someone. Now I was alone, with my drawing wooden tools in the backpack. Three or four times a week, I got down from the minibus in front of Casa Scinteii and took bus 335 to Delfinului Square, where I would continue walking on a wide boulevard bordered by rows of ten floor blocks of flats.

In the morning, along the boulevard I would walk past shops open at the ground floor of the apartment blocks in the former living rooms and bedrooms of the owners that sometimes still had the ceiling light in the middle of the ceiling, that you could enter going up the stairs built on the sidewalk, past hair saloons functioning in the hallways of apartment blocks and past the kiosks aligned on the green areas. In the evening, after eight hours of still life drawing or the construction of isometric orthogonal axonometry without a quarter, in front of the shops there were groups of people seated in a row on chairs they brought from home watching passers-by or playing backgammon, and I would take the bus and then the minibus and when it was dark outside I was back in my hometown.

Wired

In the very beginning, Bucharest was a trolleybus. Seated on our bags, we would wait for ours. Scores of trolleybuses and buses would come and we could see them from afar, before they would take the turn near the park. We looked for the metallic plate number, and if we missed it because of too many heads chocking, there was another chance to spot it sideways, in a dimly lit oval, right next to the middle door. Here it comes, I told you that must be ours, I recognized the way it moved, more like crawling really. Trolley 93 was in fact a big bus with bellows in the middle, the kind we had at home, only it was connected to some wires on top and the purr of the engine was different. The trolley advanced slowly, it was a long way and I was looking out on the window. Whenever I got a seat above a wheel, I would laugh out loud when I was thrown off the seat as it hit a hole in the street or the brakes. Before reaching our station, the trolley would almost emp-

ty, and there everybody would get down. Past the station and the market, I would go up the tenth floor of C7bis block, where I ate aubergine salad.

The kitchen had a window onto a narrow interior courtyard where echoed voices and cutlery thrown on the table and from time to time the noise of the elevator's mechanism that resembled the one made by the trolley engine.

The game

After Bucharest became a trolley and a block of flats, I began walking to my cousin's place. We left in the morning and came back in the evening. They lived one bus station further, in D10 block. Their block only had four floors and there was a communicating stairway in the front and back. Here we would

20

play in his room with small metallic cars or table football and sometimes outdoors, when he would borrow me his bike for a short ride around the block.

My cousin was a professional football player back then and he once let me play with him and the guys from the neighborhood. I was in his team, he

told me to run at all times. The field was on the street between his block and the next one, with one gate onto the heating station and the other one made of rocks. I didn't know the other boys and tried hard to give my best, I was quite nervous and there was my granny watching from the side as well. They were talking among them and calling each other on their names. They called me Carol's cousin. On our way back to C7bis I discussed with my granny the important moments in the game. She told me I did well and all the time she held in her hand a wallet and a fabric bag neatly folded. In the meantime Bucharest grew and became a big town, with Piedonne movies and crowded swimming places and jeans stores, with other trolleys and many, many other blocks and just one old house from the center, where I entered following a girl. After that Bucharest became study material for school and I became an architect.

Alex and Cristi were born in Ploiesti, in 1979. Ploiesti is a city situated 60 km North of Bucharest. Since 1998, Alex and Cristi live and work in Bucharest. In the last 12 years Cristi lived in 10 places in Bucharest and since 2003 he has a Bucharest ID. In the last 12 years Alex lived in 7 places in Bucharest and his ID address is still the one in Ploiesti city. In 2006 Alex and Cristi founded studioBASAR.

PART TWO

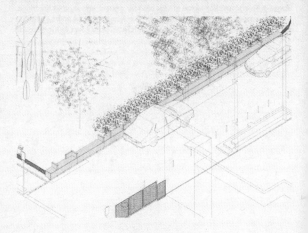

The Letter Bench

The bench is placed at the non-conflict limit between the inaccessible legal green square and the abusive parking spot on the alley, as a linear, discrete intervention that uses the existing elements: it sits on the concrete curb and it's tied to the metal fence. The backrests recall an image specific to a bookstore, suggesting a rack of books viewed from the side. The structure of the bench consists of wooden planks, and the covering is made of *Tego* left apparent (it is a material used for concrete forms, and we chose to use it because of its resistance to weather conditions and acts of vandalism). Our strategy consisted in a "performative" take on things: we did not make any presumptions about what would follow and we anticipated the dynamic of the conflict through an intervention. Surprise: due to the non-conflict nature of the area in which we placed the bench (it was not a street or a square or a sidewalk), the two irreconcilable states have peacefully co-existed since June 2009. Thus, the object led to a temporary armistice, a tacit understanding.

CREDITS   The object was made in 2009 and 2010, on the occasion of the annual urban culture event *Street Delivery*, supported by The Romanian Order of Architects.

The Generator

The intervention is part of an action focused on a case study: an Urban Island in Aviației District, where we initiated several public debates in the form of Extraordinary Meetings of the Tenants, and where we presented to the actual beneficiaries the principles developed during *The Magic Blocks* workshop. During such meetings, we also promoted the first intervention in the area, i.e. the Generator of Public Space: a multi-purpose, modular, OSB object, with a temporary life, but with possibilities of relocation within the precincts of the block. The proposal "was adopted," and the object-gift was placed in the first, linear situation, on the side of an "access gate" inside the island of blocks, on a non-conflict limit which was not reclaimed by anyone: a concrete step, a constructive remnant joined to the massive rear wall.

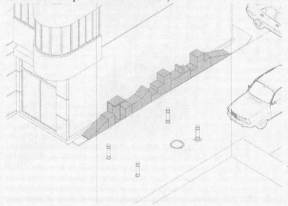

P.S.¹   After almost 9 months of non-conflict location, the Generator was removed by force, falling victim to an action of landscape cleaning and improvement and leaving behind a non-community space and disappointed inhabitants.

P.S.²   The Generator found a new use, contributing to the activation of another public place within the *Magic Blocks 2010* intervention.

CREDITS   The object was made in October 2009, following the invitation of the *Magic Blocks* project.

The Sparrow Tree

We put up an OSB structure, like a red cape enveloping the phone booth, turning it into a temporary stopover: a platform with a place where to sit, to listen to the city and observe it. Once you entered the pavilion geometrically delineated in the midst of the urban congestion, you could listen at the still operational public telephone to the history of a name – *The Sparrow Tree*, which referred, in the past, to the area around the University Fountain, a story forgotten now. We thus asserted the need to recover and document the minor memory, which also pertains to a place laden with monuments and

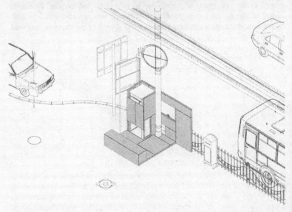

major emotional symbols, as well as the need to promote a new attitude with respect to design in the public space. The structure became in turn a shelter for homeless people, a place of rest for the beggars hanging around Magheru Boulevard traffic lights, a place where passers-by can meet, have a chat or stop for a while.

CREDITS   The installation was part of the *Ars Telefonica* project, curated by Alina Şerban, Anca Benera, Arnold Estefan and Cătălin Rulea, 23/27.09.2008 at the Centre for Visual Introspection.

The Totem

The site of the intervention consisted in a corner pillar belonging to the fence of the bookstore, a parking metal pillar and the space in between. The require-

24

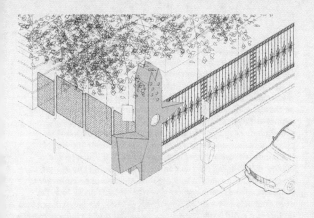

ments of the theme – an urban signal for the *Street Delivery* event, but also the special location – the former entrance to the property (the house used to be a private residence, the pioneers' centre, a bookstore, a tea house), determined an intervention of the type figurative Totem, with a multi-purpose role. Covering the fence pillar and propped by the metal pipe, the installation object cumulated four functions: cage for a dog (a stray dog or a watch dog), a street advertising board (the original pillar and the car traffic sign already pointed to this urban need), informative plate (a signaling arrow marking the start of the Verona pedestrian portion) and collective bird cribs. The structure was quickly referred to by the work team as "Pupăza din Tei" (the Hoopoe in the Lime Tree) as the boards were carved in a workshop in "Lacul Tei" (The Lake of the Lime Tree) district. Thus the intervention started its career as an urban mascot, and is programmed to be relocated, in the future, to the Girls' School, where pupils will take hold of it.

CREDITS   The object was made in 2010, on the occasion of the annual urban culture event *Street Delivery,* supported by The Romanian Order of Architects

"THIS TOWN IS ABOUT TO CHANGE"

(H&M advertising banners in Bucharest, March 2011)

RUMOURS

– "Sisters, we won!!! My source (a good one) confirms what we've been all hearing for a long time, but it seemed too good to be true: H&M reaches Romania." (Oana Dobre, journalist, on her blog, September 2007)

– "Following Marks & Spencer, Debenhams, Zara and C&A, H&M is supposedly next to enter the local market. Romania seems to be definitely on the fashion giants' map." (Business Magazin, May 24, 2010)

– "I keep hearing from everybody about H&M coming to Romania, but sadly I can't see that yet." (Business Magazin, May 24, 2010)

PRODUCTION

– "H&M entered Romania with Lohn orders since 1993."
– "We ship around 2 million pieces per year to H&M. Since the beginning of last year we gave up Lohn and only work integral products." (Iuliana Dinoiu, Romanita Company, Caracal ;In Dialog textil, September 9, 2010)
– "H&M is a brand with high expectations as to the pay levels, working standards, work safety, employees' rights etc." (Dialog Textil, September 9, 2010)
– "If someone finds it strange to see Made in Romania labels on H&M clothes bought in the West, how is it when you buy them from China?" (Valentina comment on Mihai Morar's blog, April 16, 2007)

PERCEPTION H&M

- "Madonna advertises *APACA textile workers*" (HotNews, Mihai Morar blog, April 16, 2007); the quote appeared during Madonna for H&M campaign 2007, APACA being an iconic platform for textile production in Romania.
- "In Romania, the company automatically targets a medium high public because a) it comes from the Western world and b) an H&M shirt costs more than one bought in the nearby store that says *Thread and Shuttle Co. – pieces of clothing for men* (comment Mailman on Mihai Morar's blog, April 17, 2007)
- "The coming in Romania of H&M, the biggest fashion chain in the world would be a vote of confidence on a long term regarding the developing potential of the market." (Business Magazin, May 24, 2010)

UNOFFICIAL RETAIL NETWORKS :
FACTORY SURPLUS,
SECOND – HAND AND OUTLET

– "Miniprix sells clothes from Zara and H&M – with the label cut off. You can also try at this anonymous little shop on Mendeleev street, near Amzei Square that has an "outlet" in the Press House, second floor, under the name of *Auntie Veta* (www.supersale.ro, March 2011)

– "Caracal, the city of wonders, became one of the favourite destinations for shopping addicts in the South of the country."

– "The woman knows the little secret of the discount prices, as all Romanita clients know: the factory outlet sells faulty clothes, that is products with small defects that will not be allowed to be exported in the chain stores all over the world" (Evenimentul Zilei newspaper, September 2008)

H&M OPENING
BUCHAREST
<u>MARCH 25, 2011</u>

&M DIXIT:

"THIS TOWN IS ABOUT TO CHANGE" (advertising ...ners in Bucharest, March 2011)

...IRST H&M STORE OPENS IN ROMANIA. AROUND ...00 H&M FANS WAITING AT AFI PALACE ...TROCENI", Karl-Johan Persson, CEO, and Carlos ...rte, Country Manager Romania, cut the ...ugural red ribbon together with the two store ...nagers, Alina Cristea and Doina Bunea. (March ... 2011)

...Ve feel a warm welcome from our Romanian ...comers, who can finally shop fashion and ...lity at the best price at H&M", says Carlos ...rte, H&M Romania Country Manager (March 29, ...1)

...y the end of spring 2011, H&M will open 5 ...e stores, 4 in Bucharest and one in Brasov. ... stores will open in Cluj and Timisoara during ...autumn." (March 29, 2011)

ROMANIAN PRESS ABOUT
H&M OPENING

- "It was just like when McDonalds's came in Romania, back in 1995" (Bogdan Naumovici, advertising guru in Evenimentul Zilei newspaper, March 25, 2011)
- "This morning only a handful of newspapers didn't show H&M advertising. On TV, the Swedish retailer pumped huge sums of money in buying generous advertising space. For a week now Unirii metro station, the main metro traffic junction in the city has been wrapped in H&M posters. (Evenimentul Zilei newspaper, March 25, 2011)

- Launch of H&M store in AFI Palace Cotroceni mall – FIGURES
1 of 3 visitors male
700 people at all time in the shop
700–800 people at all time queuing
30–40 guards watching the rows of clients
(Evenimentul Zilei newspaper, March 25, 2011)

- "The first H&M store opened in Sweden in 1947. There are over 2,200 H&M stores in over 38 countries all over the world. The group employs around 87,000 people and made a net profit in 2010 of around 2 billion dollars." (Capital magazine, March 25, 2011)
- "What are the chances of Romanian brands to enter Romanians' conscience after H&M?" (Paula Nemea, chief editor Shopping Report)

- "I've been buying H&M the last few years, from Spain and Austria. They are lasting clothes. They are not cheap, but they last" (George Bogos, 33 years old in Evenimentul Zilei newspaper, March 25, 2011)
- "I can hardly wait to see this promotion campaign over. I see Gisele Bundchen (French model, image of the latest H&M campaign) more often that I see my friends and family. She's everywhere", says Roxana, 27 years old (Ziarul Financiar newspaper, March 21, 2011)
- "39,9 and 89,9 lei is all I remember from this campaign" (Ziarul Financiar newspaper, March 21, 2011)
- "H&M comes and conquers everything" (Paula Negrea, chief editor Shopping Report)

ROMANIAN FASHION DESIGNERS

"In time, H&M in Romania will have a positive effect on designers, when people will realize a new uniform has been adopted." (Andra Clitan)

"There will be an *appetite* for combining designer pieces with basics. Moreover, people might become aware of the importance of owning a unique design piece versus mass produced design pieces." (Adelina Ivan)

"I won't have to fly to Milano or Paris to buy accessories for photo shootings. (Ludmila Corlateanu)

&M is a sort of IKEA in clothing." (Smaranda Almasan)

CREDITS

All images and texts by the authors
except the following:

(A) pp. 26,27
Photos by Ioana Pârvan
for CIRCA 1703 - 3071, Bucharest

(G) pp. 98,100,101
Text by Ilinca Micu. Excerpt from the
artist book *Noah's Ark–An Improbable
Space Survival Kit*, authors: Corina Ilea
& Ştefan Constatinescu (Arvinius +
OrfeusPublishing, Stockholm, 2021).

(M) pp. 157,162
Photos by Horaţiu Şovăialā
pp. 163
Photo by Andrei Becheru
pp. 164-165
Photos by Virginia Lupu

(P) pp. 218
*The Impossibility of Counting
That Which is Without Number*
29 x 21 cm, ink, coffee, lipstick on paper,
2015
pp. 219
Devil Is An Ugly Crier
21 x 15 cm, markers on paper, 2016
pp. 220-221
Misty
100 x 140 cm, graphite powder and baby
oil on paper, 2014
pp. 222
Flowers Growing Out of My Chest 2
130 x 130 cm, pencil, ballpoint pen and
marker on paper, 2019
pp. 223
Flowers Growing Out of My Chest 3
120 x 110 cm, pencil and marker on paper,
2019
pp. 224
Prolly God
20 x 15 cm, marker on paper, 2016

(S) pp. 250
Illustration by Valentina Bin

(T) pp. 257, 258, 262-263
Photos by Irina Botea

(Y) pp. 304-311
All photos by Juergen Teller & Venetia
Scott, Romania 1990

The editors graciously thank all the
awesome contributing artists, architects,
researchers, writers, the publisher PUNCH
(Radu Lesevschi) and to the following:
Josh Plough
Serioja Bocsok
Otilia Mihalcea Fiastru Eugen Vasile
Mihnea Mircan
Maria Farcaş
Erika Olea
Marin Olea
Ruxandra Demetrescu
Daniela Calciu
Elena Morariu
Christine and Elsa König
Diane Pernet
Florin Madar
Liviana Dan
Irina Nemţeanu
Laura Paraschiv / CIRCA 1703 -3071
Anca Mihuleţ Kim
Alain Servais
Eva Ruiz
Mareike Dittmer
Dirk De Wit
Danielle van Zuijlen
Veronica & Maria Szabo
Letizia Ragaglia
Frida Carazzato
Anna Chiţan
Mihai Mihalcea
Josselin Merazguia
Mihaela Harsan

The publisher would also like to thank
all contributors and
Dragoş Olea
Erika Olea
Sandra Demetrescu
Ioana Nemeş
Josh Plough
Irina Cios
Carmen Constantin
Mihaela Păun
Cristina Cioran
Eugen Vasile
Kaido Raat
Mihai Mihalcea
Eugenia & Valeriu
and everyone else who made this
publication possible.